LET'S MOVE IN TOGETHER

LET'S MOVE IN TOGETHER

Enhancing the Joy of Co-Living

To Hazza & Alex,
May your lives together be more joy-filled than you ever thought possible
Papa

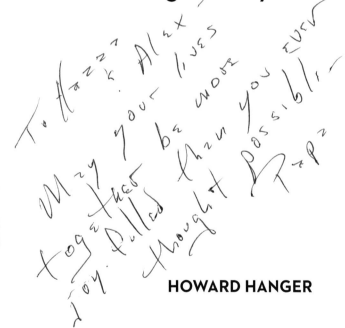

HOWARD HANGER

Cover Design by Don Pedi

ISBN: 978-1-940858-42-5
Proudly Printed in the United States of America

Asheville, North Carolina, USA
ashevillejill1@gmail.com

Dedicated to Hanger Hall, my home. The grand old girl saved my life by giving me something to live for; and I, in turn saved her life by keeping her from the wrecking ball. She has blessed me and blissed me; and over the years given hundreds of people a safe, secure and happy home.

WHO IS HOWARD HANGER?

As one reviewer put, "Howard Hanger is more of a verb than a noun." And his life bears that out. Having studied under Dr. Margaret Mead, Howard graduated from Emory University (BA in Anthropology) and from Candler School of Theology (MDiv in Sociology of Religion.) He was - after six years of being put on hold – ordained in the United Methodist Church and appointed to Experimental Ministries Beyond the Local Church. Howard took that ordination seriously and has never stopped experimenting.

He travelled with his band, first called "Howard Hanger Trio" and then "Jazz Fantasy" when the band members numbered five or more. In The States, he crisscrossed the Country playing in schools – elementary to college – and then travelled twelve years with the Department of Defense to 26 countries around the world. Howard always took pride in knowing that at least a part of the U.S. defense budget was going to music. With his band, Howard has recorded fourteen albums.

In 1993, he bought an 1890s Victorian mansion and developed a living cooperative which has been operating since and is currently home to fourteen people. Which is what this book is all about.

In 1989, he founded Jubilee! Community, a multi-faith spiritual gathering which has continued to thrive to this day. His book, "The Main Thing" is the story of Jubilee! http://www.jubileecommunity.org/

In 1999, he started Hanger Hall – A School for Girls, the first independent school for middle school girls in Asheville, North Carolina, which continues to prosper. His book with co-author, Dr. Vicki Garlock, "A Precious Window of Time," chronicles the School's development and philosophy. http://www.hangerhall.org/#

Howard has two daughters and two granddaughters and continues as full-time minister of Jubilee! Community. A popular wedding officiant, Howard presides over 60-80 weddings each year. Best-selling author Tom Robbins ("Still Life With Woodpecker," "Jitterbug Perfume," "Skinny Legs and All" and many others) writes, "Howard's goal – the goal whether they can articulate it or not – of all who truly follow a spiritual path, is to become, in the words of Joseph Campbell 'translucent to the transcendent.'" www.howardhanger.com

CONTENTS

INTRODUCTION

Having lived in and operated a shared housing cooperative since 1973, I have learned a few things about living with other people. I certainly don't have the answers or all the how-tos, but along the way I have stumbled upon – far more stumble than intention – many things that work and don't work for folks who want to live together.

Now a bit of clarity. The title of this opus – "Let's Move In Together" -- could be understood as a manual for romantic relationships. Au contraire, mon amour. Though there may be a certain romance in living with other unrelated people, you'll have to find your guidance for amorous live-in situations elsewhere. There are similarities. Love & lust-oriented or not, moving in together requires more than a bit of commitment and responsibility. Be that as it may, this handbook will do you precious little good if it's only you and your hottie moving in together.

Nor is this a manual for co-housing. Co-housing is a cluster of private homes usually around a shared space which may include a clubhouse for anyone in the community to use for parties, extra guests or whatever. Members of a co-housing community share with each other and support each other, but they live separately.

What we're talking about here is multiple folks living together under one roof. Sometimes they're related, but mostly not. It can be called a 'housing cooperative', 'living cooperative', 'shared housing,' 'commune,' 'intentional community,' or simply 'living with roommates.' A housing cooperative can be a legal entity in which the unrelated members of the household own shares of the property and jointly live in and maintain the home.

The Living Cooperative of which I am a part is called Hanger Hall and is not a legal entity. Hanger Hall (didn't stay awake all night coming up with the name) started in 1973, when I bought a gorgeous 1890 Victorian mansion which was condemned, falling down and on track to be demolished. Plans were to take it down and build a warehouse for welding equipment. The thought of that possibility still gives me the willies. Instead, my band (Jazz Fantasy) and I moved from Detroit – a great place to move from – and settled inside its deteriorating walls. Actually, the walls were fine -- the ceilings and floors -- not so much. With seven or eight moon-sized craters in the roof, when it rained, we had regular showers in every room though with nary a scrap of working indoor plumbing. Water came through the roof, but not out of the faucets.

The leaks in the house stopped pretty quickly with a new roof; but it took us four years to bring the old girl up to code. There was no kitchen when we moved in. The servants' kitchen in the basement (hard to find good servants these days) had long since been dismantled; so we built a new one along with a passive solar addition.

Restoring an old house is an enormous challenge, aka a wallet buster. But with lots of stripping (woodwork), scraping, sanding, dry-walling, wiring, plumbing, and maxing out several credit cards with appliances, light fixtures, tubs, sinks, windows, furnaces and heaters, the place became -- and still is -- not only livable, but utterly loveable.

- Lesson 1 -

Sometimes finding and creating the perfect place for your cooperative living can be an exhausting and expensive pain in the butt. Don't let it stop you.

In the meantime, my band, along with various girlfriends and boyfriends moved in and out, each paying their rent mostly with manual labor. It was work. Hard-ass work. And many days and nights, we would drink or smoke our exhaustion away. We did add a hot-tub early on. We were musicians, after all. First things first.

So after a few years, it began to dawn on us that we had created a shared housing/living cooperative/housing cooperative. Call it what you will, we had created a home for people who wanted to live with other people. The initial intent was not to start a living cooperative but simply to provide a place for my band to live and rehearse when we weren't on the road. And it worked well in that regard.

Soon after the renovations, word spread that there was a Victorian mansion with a hot-tub where you could rent a room. And our rooms (now 29 total with 15 bedrooms) filled quickly and have stayed that way ever since. Over the years, we have had hundreds of people who have lived at The Hall. Mostly equally split between men and women. We've had gay, straight and bi-. We've had black and white. Average age has run around 40. Average stay, about 5-7 years. One of our current residents has been with us since the early 80s.

In the mid-80s, I got married. My (then) wife was fortunately very comfortable living with multiple people and we had two delightfully amazing daughters. And we soon discovered that a live-in village does indeed help to raise a child. As our daughters got older and went to friends' homes to play, they began to realize what a unique situation they had. And for the most part, they enjoyed it.

Over the years, we have added more rooms, upgraded bathrooms, built a new kitchen, added solar-heated hot water, increased insulation, put on another new roof, painted the whole thing several times and installed a good-sized in-ground swimming pool.

- Lesson 2 -

Never... I say, NEVER EVER install a swimming pool
unless you can afford professional maintenance.
Yet another of life's hard - and expensive -- lessons.

Along the way we have also experimented with different patterns of living, working, and sharing together. We have had house meetings (not at all productive), assigned jobs (even less so), developed rotating job wheels with job assignments changing weekly (utter disaster), house meals (huge successes), house game nights (moderate success), hot-tub parties (not for the shy), volley ball games (great for some), experimented with the purchase of shared items: toilet paper, light bulbs, potatoes, onions, flour, sugar, butter, half & half, cleaning goods, etc. All these items today are included in the rent.

We have tried and failed over and over; but in the process, we have weeded out the worthless modes of living together and nurtured the worthy. After four decades you should sure as hell learn a few things. And, of course, we are still learning. Not all of the ideas in this manual may work for you; but they have worked for many hundreds of Hanger Hallians for a long, long time.

Living with people who like to live with other people can be exceptionally rewarding and tremendously challenging. It opens each person to other ways of thinking and operating on this planet. It provides a potent and irreplaceable connection to other souls, other minds, other joys, other sorrows. And it offers true community -- one of the national deficits we have today and one of our greatest human needs.

Let's Move in Together!

I moved into Hanger Hall shortly
after finding out about my Mother's ovarian cancer diagnosis,
she lived another year and a half
and her death had a deep impact on me.
I found great comfort in knowing
that this community of people
whom I loved
and who loved me
were right outside my door.
Through that time, I learned
that I did not always need to engage
with anyone in the kitchen
or common areas,
sometimes a nod or a wave,
an occasional hug,
was enough to express our mutual respect
and love and support of one another.
Not that it was without frustration or challenges,
but at that time
it was a huge gift
that I did not feel alone in my grief.

Addy Wygmans, 2012-2015

CHAPTER 1

Cooperative Living, Cooperative Housing, Communal Living, Shared Housing... What's what?

ONEIDA COMMUNITY – THE GREAT EXPERIMENT

John Humphrey Noyes was a man who believed in perfection. Christian perfection. Big time Christian perfection. In every aspect of life. He believed people could not only achieve perfection, but by living together –sinless, in union with God –help each other toward that goal. He was the founder of Oneida –arguably, the most successful utopian socialist community in the United States. Oneida was clear and unambiguous communal living.

Located in Oneida, New York, with 300 members at its zenith, each person shared everything: food, possessions, religious fervor and... sexual partners. With their concept of "complex marriage" (as if marriage isn't complex enough), every man in Oneida was married to every woman and every woman married to every man. Having sex with someone was based solely on mutual consent. Multiple partners were encouraged as a way to end jealousy and envy. Noyes taught that lovemaking brought partners closer to each other and to God. "Our Communities," Noyes declared, "are families as distinctly bounded and separated from promiscuous society as ordinary households. The tie that binds us together is as permanent and sacred, to say the least, as that of common marriage, for it is our religion." (From *The Noyes Plays: The True History of The Oneida Community*). In some ways, Oneida made the 60's sexual revolution look like a Baptist Sunday School picnic with the possible exception that the members of Oneida abstained from alcohol, drugs, tobacco, profanity, and obscenity. OK, a little like a Baptist picnic.

Noyes, born September 3, 1811, in Brattleboro, Vermont, graduated from Dartmouth College and attended Andover Theological Seminary and Yale Theological College. He became convinced that through religious practices and self-will, anyone could live a perfectly balanced and sin-free life. He took Jesus at his word that the Kingdom of Heaven was here and now and we simply had to find our place in that kingdom.

The community lived in a huge mansion (93,000 square feet) which they gradually built and expanded over the years. The goal was noble: to demonstrate that people can live in peace together in a way that no one goes without. The idea of Oneida was to become the seed of a society and world where there was justice and equality for all. It was the American dream on steroids.

Eager to get his ideas out to anyone who would listen, Noyes published several books; *The Berean* (1847), *Bible Communism* (1848), *Male Continence* (1848), *Scientific Propagation* (1873), *Home Talks* (1875) and *History of American Socialisms* (1870). But worldwide acceptance of his views was not to be. Public outrage built in the 1870's until Noyes fled to Canada for fear of being prosecuted for sex related crimes. In 1881, the Oneida Community abandoned their socialist/perfectionist ideology and opened a manufacturing business in which the former members of the Community became shareholders. The focus of Oneida shifted from big-time perfection to big bucks. The Oneida Corporation is still a successful producer of flatware and other household items.

Noyes kept his dream alive for 33 years. But the dream of living together in a kind of utopia continues to be an aspiration that has tantalized parts of civilization for a long time. We human bozos have lived as tribes and clans, bound together by ancestors, customs, ethnicity and tradition as far back as anthropologists can dig. Whether the purpose was security, shared tasks, food, shelter, propagation or whatever, we two-leggeds have continually found that living together was mostly better than living alone. Mostly. And the only way to live together successfully has been to cooperate. AKA sharing. Cooperative living, cooperative or shared housing, is based on collaboration, teamwork, partnership and, you guessed it, cooperation and sharing.

*Oneida Community Collection in the Syracuse Library. *Syracuse, New York, Department of Special Collections, 1998*

THE FARM

The Farm, located on three square miles in central Tennessee, has been operating as an intentional community since 1971. Some several hundred followers of a counter-culture Haight-Ashbury hippie named Steven Gaskin, moved to an abandoned farm and devoted themselves to following a peaceful and spiritual path. Gaskin authored over a dozen books, was a political activist and even ran for the U.S. presidency in 2000 on the Green Party ticket.

The Farm still continues as a community of about 200 folks —families and individuals who strive to live in concert with the earth, work with each other and (in the words of their website) "to make the world a better place". The Farm hosts an "EcoVillage Training

Center," designed to teach natural building techniques, perma-culture gardening and sustainable living. They also host a Midwifery Center focusing on natural birthing with prenatal education, labor coaching and postpartum care.

Now, in their 45th year, the leaders and members of the community continue to value the ideals of living close to the land, non-violent communication, sustainability, because (again in the words of their website) "by living together in community, individuals gain greater leverage in the pursuit of their ideals."

Further info: thefarmcommunity.org

BIOLOGY OF COOPERATION

Cooperation and sharing are not, however, simply behaviors espoused by googly-moogly-starry-eyed-uber-optimists. Cooperation and sharing are looped and helixed into our DNA. In fact, without cooperation and sharing on the biological level, life could simply not exist.

Cassandra Extavour, a developmental biologist at Harvard, has studied how healthy living cells share and cooperate. When a mammal is developing in the womb, for example, stem cells are wildly differentiating. Liver cells are becoming a liver; heart cells, a heart; eye cells, an eye. And as soon as any particular part of the body is finished, the stem cells stop creating. Otherwise, the liver might grow to the size of a watermelon or the eye, a volley ball. Then for the body's sustenance and maintenance, cells must continue to cooperate and share with each other for healing and growth to happen. In other words, cells are willing to let go of their initial function and cooperate for a greater good.

In other words, you and I could not have developed or evolved into whoever we are without cooperation on a very basic cellular level.

Cancer cells, on the other hand, do not cooperate. They don't know when to stop and they do not share. Rather than cooperating with other cells around them, they preempt and take over other living cells. Even entire organs. And unless the cancer cells are stopped, they will literally devour a body and then die in the process. Cooperation is absolutely essential for life to exist.

There are hermits, of course. Recluse loners, outsiders, ascetics. There are those of us who prefer solitude to community. Nor is solitude necessarily an uncooperative choice.

Julian of Norwich, who lived in the late 14th and early 15th centuries, was an anchoress. Anchorites were those who had chosen to withdraw from human society for the purpose of intense prayer and contemplation. They would live alone in small cells - not a stem cell —which were sometimes attached to a church or cathedral. We don't even know Julian's real name. We simply know that she lived out her life in a cell built into the wall of the Church of St. Julian in Norwich, England.

Nor was Julian's retreat from society a negative reflection on humanity. In truth, in absenting herself from the social structure of the day, she was cooperating in her own way. Through thought, prayer, reflection, meditation and writing, she was able to share her wisdom gathered in solitude and thus enhance the lives of the world she had chosen to absent. Julian's most famous teaching is "All shall be well and all shall be well and all manner of things shall be well." It's an affirmation of faith... an affirmation that can keep you going when things aren't going so well.

But most folks don't choose the solitary life. Even though we all enjoy alone time, there is a big drive within each of us to be in some way connected to other people. We enjoy all kinds of interaction —mental, emotional, spiritual, physical. We like to bounce our ideas off other brains and learn new ways of seeing life we may not have considered. We like to laugh together, share feelings and when the tears flow, we know there's nothing like a friendly shoulder and some comforting wrap-around arms. And like Noyes... Mr. Oneida, himself... we are still exploring ways of helping people connect with each other to enrich the lives of everyone.

ORGANIZED STUDENT COOPERATIVES

NASCO - North American Students of Cooperation - is an outfit that has been around since 1968. Their avowed purpose is "to educate and organize an emerging generation of cooperators." The idea behind their mission is that we can do things together that we cannot do on our own. And by "promoting a community oriented cooperative movement," NASCO hopes to help people help people.

Like Noyes, NASCO and other like organizations are idealistic and practical at the same time. Unlike Noyes, NASCO does not advocate total socialism, religious conviction or multiple sex partners. But the goal is essentially the same: learning to live and work together so as to make this world a more lively and livable place.

There are all kinds of organizations and corporations which promote cooperative living. The CLO (Cooperative Living Organization) in Gainesville, Florida, is one of the oldest of such outfits. Begun in 1932, by four boys who decided to live together in a garage apartment and pool their resources and labor so they could afford to stay in college. The group quickly expanded to more than 20 members. They rented other housing, elected a governing board and called themselves the Collegiate Living Association. By 1938, over 60 were part of the Association. And as of 2016, they are still hopping and (according to their website) conveniently located behind the Chipotle Grill. There are worse locations for college students.

The criteria for membership is financial need, academic achievement and willingness to share equally in expenses and work as a group. The CLO continues to operate successfully and is now associated with NASCO (mentioned earlier). Like the Oneida Community, CLO is committed to the notion that living together provides possibilities and potential for the entire community —possibilities that living alone could never provide.

There are plenty of folks, of course, who find ways of living cooperatively together without the help or guidance of any formal organization. There are plenty of people who rent and live together, or buy and live together without the assistance of any outside organization. But the mere fact that these cooperative living organizations exist and thrive is a clear testimony that John Humphrey Noyes was onto something; something that many people not only desire, but find very helpful in navigating the waters of living.

SEEKING TOGETHERNESS

Most of us spend the first years of our lives with our "nuclear family." Mom and/or Dad. Or Mom and Mom or Dad and Dad. Some of us are farmed out to grandparents or relatives and some into "homes" for safety or security. But our initial living experience, whether positive or negative, is almost always with other people around. And perhaps that is what we try to emulate after we leave the nuclear home with roommates, lovers, housemates, hook-ups, spouses and friends. We join dance groups and classes, bowling teams and pick-up basketball games. We attend churches, synagogues, covens or some sort of dance-naked-in-the-woods-find-God-in-ganja spiritual group. (God and ganja do, after all, begin with the same letter. Coincidence?) We go hiking, running, biking with folks who share our interests and passions. And then there are the concerts and major sporting events where we join with thousands of people who share what brings us delight.

It is clear that no matter how good or bad our childhood family experiences might have been, we still crave connection with other people. Deep within us, we still harbor the ancient tribe or clan mentality that urges us to be together with other people.

INTENTIONAL COMMUNITIES

One of the main differences, of course, between Noyes' outfit and NASCO or like organizations is the difference in intent. Any so-called "intentional community" usually has some kind of mission statement to which all members subscribe. It could be a religious or spiritual intention, an environmental intention, or some intention focusing on moral or ethical issues. But the truth is, whether stated or not, every cooperative living situation has an intent.

If two women meet at work, for example, and decide to move in together, the intent may be to

- Save money
- Provide a sense of security
- Stem loneliness
- Become lovers
- Afford a nicer or more convenient place
- Enhance a burgeoning friendship
- Share pet care

...or any of a dozen other possibilities. But whether stated or not, if these women decide to live together there is some intention behind it. Every cooperative living arrangement is an intentional community. And the intent need not all be the same.

One of the women, for example, may have just gotten out of a relationship and craves companionship in the evenings. Her new housemate, however, simply feels safer not living alone and is very happy to have a companion. Two different intentions: one intentional community.

And yes, a community can be as small as 2-3 or as large as you make it. Admittedly, 2, 3 or 4 people living together usually call themselves "roommates" or "housemates." But once you begin actually living together, the dynamics are the same no matter what the number. The challenges, the fun, the day-to-day maintenance and shared expenses are all the same no matter if there are 2 or 12 living together.

My experience is that once you get above around 12 people living together, however, patterns shift and change significantly. 12 seems to be a magical number, at least in my experience. 12 signs of the Zodiac, 12 tribes of Israel, 12 disciples of Jesus, 12 months of the year, 12 Days of Christmas... something going on there. Once you get too far above 12 persons in community, however, an impersonality begins to sneak in. All of a sudden, you are relating to the group instead of the individual. You feel part of an institution rather than a community. We have had as many as 19 living together in our house. We won't do that again. I cannot fathom how Noyes did it with 300. Maybe it was religious focus. Maybe it was the free sex.

For our purposes in this little manual we define shared or cooperative housing as 3 or more unrelated individuals (though some may be partners) who have:

- chosen to live under the same roof,
- enjoy living in community or at least are willing to try,
- may or may not have individual private rooms,
- share kitchen, bathrooms and other common spaces, and
- share in the costs of maintaining the home.

In so many ways leaving Indiana
just as I was turning 21 and moving
into Hanger Hall ---and to Asheville
was really the launching pad of my life!
Those years living at Hanger Hall were certainly some
of the most formative .. exciting .. mind blowing ..
sometimes difficult and intimidating
(to this sheltered preacher's daughter from Indiana).

THE MOST INTERESTING people came to live and to visit..
really never a dull moment!...and 42 years later,
I continue to feel so fortunate
to have been invited into a house
full of some of the most
creative, quirky, hilarious human beings I've ever known.

Beth Youngblood, 1974 - 1982

CHAPTER 2

SHARING AND RESPECT

SHARING SPACE

As a child, did you ever get a report card on which your teacher had written "plays well with other children" or something of the sort? Or..."Johnny needs to learn to keep his hands to himself and not bring firecrackers in his backpack?" If you "played well with other children," and have kept up that trait into adulthood, you are a good candidate for cooperative housing. If, on the other hand, you were the pushy, fire-cracker kid and have continued in that pattern, you might be better served living as a Buddhist nudist hermit in a Mongolian yurt, a tree-house, or at the very least in a far-removed one-bedroom bungalow.

Playing together and sharing are what makes shared cooperative living, well... shared and cooperative. And fun. It's what makes it even possible. It's the interaction, the many ways you interface with your living companions that truly makes co-op living come alive. Yes, co-op living can save you money. Yes, it lessens loneliness and bumps up security. But, when you find yourself around a dinner table talking trash or philosophy—or philosophic trash—and you find yourselves roaring together in laughter, or when you group-hug someone in your home who is going through tough times and cry together, then the issues of money, loneliness, and security drop way down on the priority scale. It's the magic of togetherness that makes it all worthwhile; community works wonders.

And it's all about sharing and playing. Keeping it light. Keeping it fluid. Keeping it open and honest. Sort of like any successful relationship. Co-op living is, indeed, a uniquely precious connection that offers comfort, assurance, and love in ways that few other relationships can. Marriage, or any one-on-one relationship can also provide comfort, assurance, and love, along with fantastic opportunities for personal growth and stability. With co-op living, however, that same comfort, assurance, and love can come to you from several different people in several different ways. And the possibilities for personal growth and stability are exponentially bountiful. John Noyes of the Oneida Community knew that. He understood that in order to live together on this planet we simply must learn to live together. And living together—, whether on a planet or in a house, means sharing.

When you share space with other people, it means that sometimes you may go in the kitchen to make a sandwich and another person is in the kitchen popping corn. You know you don't need the whole kitchen to make your sandwich nor does your housemate need much space for his or her Orville Redenbacher munchies. (Add some butter for me, thank you.) And maybe the two of you chat; maybe you don't. Maybe you share sandwich and kernels. Maybe you don't. It doesn't matter. What matters is thinking of the kitchen as "ours," not "mine" or "yours." It's that kind of thinking which makes co-op living work. It's that kind of awareness that makes the Chief

Seattle quote—*The earth does not belong to us; we belong to the earth*— boom and sparkle like a 4th of July on steroids.

Co-op living is all about sharing: Sharing space, sharing time, sharing food, sharing an understanding that people are different and go through different moods and think in different ways and encounter different experiences. And in a co-op, a willingness to share is at once a requisite and a joy.

Now sharing has its limits, of course. Unless you live totally communal, there are mutually agreed upon boundaries in each co-op regarding what is shared and what is not. In the Oneida Community, everything was shared - financial resources, clothing, food, sex, everything. And if you want to try to establish a co-op like that, go for it. But in most co-ops I know about today, certain things are shared and others not.

In our co-op, Hanger Hall, we share all the common space - living rooms, solarium, dining areas, laundry room, kitchen, hot-tub, pool, fire pit, carriage house and all of the yard. We do **not** share

- bedroom space (no one goes into another's bedroom without permission)
- food (noone eats another's food without permission unless it's house provided, like potatoes, onions, flour, sugar, butter, half & half, etc.
- clothing. You don't just slip into someone's Speedo because you think it looks good on you. Trust me: It doesn't. As the T-shirt says, "Speedo. Makes you wish you were blind."

There's always someone in the house, of course, who wishes we shared sex. But we don't do that either. Without permission. And it's amazing that over the years, how very few romantic couples have formed from residents. Little hot-tub fun every now and then, perhaps, but very few lasting one-on-one relationships. Nonetheless, sharing, playing together and cooperation are crucial for any co-op to survive.

LIVING WITH IDIOSYNCRASIES

I've got some good news and bad news.

- First the good news: Everyone is different.
- And the bad news: Everyone is different.

Or as Tom Robbins puts it: *Our Similarities bring us to a common ground. Our Differences allow us to be fascinated by each other.* "Be yourself," wrote Oscar Wilde. "Everyone else is taken." But when you have a group of people, differences can tickle you or can bug the hell out of you.

- You've got your laid-back-it'll-all-happen-in-its-time kind of personalities and you've got the get-'er-done-and-get-'er-done-now ways of operating.
- You've got the big laughers and quiet meditators.
- Pensive book readers and avid NASCAR watchers.
- You've got gluten-free, dairy-free, meat-free, sugar-free, hormone-free, GMO-free-eaters and the omnivores who like vegetables and things that eat them. We currently have a house member who picks through our compost looking for a few still-good bites.
- Some people spend hours in the bathroom getting ready for bed or for a date or for bed with a date, while others blow through bathroom time faster than a Jewish mother can make you feel guilty.
- Some folks prefer the toilet paper to roll over the top and others prefer it under.

- Some love to have 15 varieties of shampoo and conditioner at every shower; some use cheap bath soap and call it good.

And on and on and on....

Suffice it to say that there are plenty of different strokes for plenty of different folks and the whole enchilada in cooperative living is cooperation:

1) understanding that not everyone does things like you do and
2) being willing to modify some of your own quirks.

Yes, there must be ground rules for any stable household. Cleanliness, neatness, respect for quiet times, kindness and consideration to housemates, etc. But flexibility and tolerance with individual peculiarities is crucial.

NEATNIKS & SLOBS

One of the most challenging differences in communities could be called "The Cleanliness Spectrum." There are people who have no problem living in a room piled high with old newspapers and magazines, empty CD cases (yes, a few under the age of 70 still listen to CDs), long-dead electronics, love letters, crusty lasagna plates, moldy laundry and enough dust and dog hair on the floor to knit an afghan for an Eskimo. There are other people who keep their spaces as spotlessly clean and sterile as an operating room.

Our way of dealing with these differences is simple: We keep our own rooms any way we wish; but always leave the common areas as we found them. And it is the head of the household's gig—one of the main gigs—to keep the common areas clean, neat and tidy. We're not anal about it. We don't polish the woodwork and clean the windows every day. But we do vacuum and dust the common areas weekly. We do scrub the tubs and toilets regularly. And we expect everyone to never leave any dishes, books, games, electronics, clothes—any personal items—in the common areas.

And it works! The slobs of the world can go to their own rooms and enjoy their world. The neatniks can do the same. But everyone is responsible for keeping the common areas uncluttered; and the head of household is responsible for maintaining cleanliness.

RELIGIOUS, POLITICAL, DIETARY, DRUG & DRINKING DIFFERENCES

In the beginning was the Word. And the Word was RESPECT. And when the Word becomes flesh in a community, life is GOOD.

One of the beauties of people who are drawn to community living situations tends to be people who live with respect. Offer respect. Expect respect. Very seldom in the forty-plus years of operating Hanger Hall, have I encountered more than a handful of residents who were so adamant about their political, religious, sexual and dietary views that they couldn't shut up. These few had a my-way-or-the-highway approach with their opinions and created rancor and animosity; and none of them lasted very long in the household.

Over the years, some in our household have been drinkers and druggies. We do not tolerate habitual drunkenness or constant strung out behavior. But no one pushes his or her habits of abstinence or indulgence on anyone else. We have had several recovering alcoholics in our community. In almost every case, respect for the others' way of life has been paramount. And mutual respect always works. Always. But, finally, if it's not working, if there have been discussions with no improvement and respect has gone out the window, then someone—for the sake of the community—has to make the decision for the person to go. That is the job of B.D. (Benevolent Dictator) (See Chapter 7).

I'm 34 years old and I have lived in share houses my entire life.
I actively choose it every single time over and over again.
There are so many things one can say about communal living...
Who shaved their legs in the kitchen sink?
Can we throw away the dumpster Bagels yet?
Does anyone actually know the person crashed on the couch?

But let's talk about the Highlight. The ultimate reason we're all here.
Let's say - hypothetically speaking - it is a random Tuesday evening.
Two roommates decide to have a little late-night room party
that can only result in one thing:
intensely scouring the kitchen concocting the perfect recipe –
which is of course peanut butter smash
with ice cream
topped with Kahlua.
But alas!
The power Duo fall short lacking one crucial ingredient.....
For those who have never lived in communal housing there is nothing
so sweet or sinful
as a spoonful of stolen ice cream at 3 a.m.
You try and scrape the top so no one notices ---
you borrow a bit from the vanilla
and then the mint
so as not to be too obvious.
And then you go to bed the happiest, fullest, luckiest girl in the world.

And that's what it's all about.
At Hanger Hall there's always someone who has your back.
We live in support of one another.
Sometimes we give, sometimes we take,
often we share.

We love one another.
We Inspire and show up for one another.
We hold each other in hardship and we celebrate each other's victories.
We challenge and learn from one another.
We fuck up.
We eat the ice cream.
We forgive.
We try and do better next time.
We grow faster and live exponentially richer lives
than we ever would alone.
(Some might even say it's the ice cream on a peanut butter Sundae.)

Apryl Blakeney, 2016 -

CHAPTER 3

CREATING & MAINTAINING COMMUNITY

Community is finally what it's all about.

The make or break point in any living cooperative is community—whether or not community can be established and maintained. The better the community, the happier everyone is. The stronger the community, the more respect and camaraderie blossoms within that community. The healthier the community, the more support everyone feels. And when all feel supported, all support the community.

Community, however, is not a program. It's not an operation. Not a formula. Not something that can be designed and sustained by following any kind of schedule or manual. This little manual can get you started and help you avoid some speed bumps; but the 10 Commandments of Co-op living, it's not. Community is a living organism and as such, a moving target. There are no guarantees that any of the suggestions in this chapter will create and keep your community going. But these ideas and models have worked for us at Hanger Hall ever so beautifully. Well, mostly.

It's like parenting. There are all kinds of classes, books and videos on how to be a good parent. But, finally, parents and children have to learn together just how a family works. Parents and children teach each other. Which is precisely what happens in community. Guidelines are helpful, but never the final answer.

Life is not linear. Life is not neat and tidy. Life is a dance – a dance in which toes get stepped on and stumbles happen. It's a goofy, messy dance, however, that can bring exultant joy and a sense of genuine freedom as long as the partners listen for the music and feel the beat.

Community forms and thrives on the music of sharing, compassion, forgiveness and respect. And, knowing that there will be missteps – knowing that there will be embarrassing blunders -- as long as all do their damndest to dance to that music, magic will happen.

DINNERS

"Everything you see, I owe to spaghetti."
-Sophia Loren

It's true. We are what we eat. Which may be bad news for Dung Beetles, maggots and cowbirds. But, what we eat and how we eat defines us in a way that little else can. And there is nothing better than a shared meal with friends to bump up the flavor of whatever is on your plate and enhance digestion.

Here's what we know: We all eat. We all eat regularly. We are all alive in great part because we eat. And... eating can not only satisfy 'dem taste buds and fill 'dat growling belly, eating together can be just plain fun! "People who love to eat," wrote Julia Child, "are always the best people." And there's nothing like food and laughter to bring out the best in almost anyone.

Even cooking together can bring out the fun. Slicing, dicing, stirring, tasting, trying new spices, tasting, adding untried combinations, tasting, sautéing, poaching, grilling, boiling, steaming, broiling, frying, toasting and roasting and tasting can turn a kitchen scene into a delightful and delectable culinary circus. And then, when you sit down and share the results with copious "oooohs" and "aaaaaahs," you get a little sample of heaven on earth.

At Hanger Hall, I love to cook. I take great pleasure in cruising the grocers, allowing my taste buds and wallet to decide what to bring home and prepare for the feast. Usually one or two of the Hallians will kick in and help for a bit. But with or without the sous-chef, I flip on some music...

(COSMIC TRUTH: FOOD ALWAYS TASTES BETTER WHEN IT'S PREPARED WITH MUSIC PLAYING)

...and slice and dice and all the rest. It's a kind of meditation for me. It feels ever so good to be creating something that will hopefully get that good feeling going for everyone.

And then, we eat. Meals at the Hall usually end up with 8-12 around the table – residents and guests. Not everyone, of course, is available. With classes, work, dates and vacations, we seldom have all house members at the table.

We always begin the meal by holding hands. Because of our individual religious or nonreligious preferences, we don't exactly pray. At least not in the traditional sense. Rather we offer good words. *Bene dictum*, as the Latin religios would say. It's where the word "Benediction" originates – something spoken at the end of religious ceremony. We begin our meals with Bene dictum. With good words.

Our meals come at the end of the day – no way can we get a group together for lunch, or God Forbid – breakfast. So we invite people to say anything good about the day just past. And, in the hand-holding and the thinking of good thoughts, a tangible sense of togetherness begins to gel – even when we have some guests who have never dined with us. The simple act of holding hands around the table, sharing good thoughts, with the sumptuous aromas of food which we grace as it graces us, fosters a rich sense of togetherness which little else can offer. It's like good religion. It may well be the best part of religion. Physical connection and *bone dictum*.

Another tradition of Hanger Hall dinners is what we call, "Table Questions." Anyone can offer a table question. It can relate to something you're struggling with; some new thing you want to try. It can be an ethical question, political pondering, or simply a request to share our goofiest or most embarrassing dreams.

Some of our spontaneous table questions have been:

- Describe your happiest or worst birthday party.
- If you could be any age other than what you are, what it would be?
- If you could be any age for a day and then come back, what would it be?
- What is your idea of a perfect vacation?
- What's the worst job you could ever imagine doing?
- What are three things you want to do before you die?
- What are three things you have done but wish you hadn't?
- If you could sleep with anyone from ancient history, who would it be?
- If you could have had anyone from history as your parent, who would it be?
- What's the most important life lesson you have learned so far?

...etc.

If no one has a table question ready to go, we pass around a wonderful little book called, *"If... (Questions for the Game of Life)" by Evelyn McFarlane & James Saywell, Villard Press.* This fun little book has hundreds and hundreds of scintillating conversation starters. OK, they aren't all scintillating. Some are ho-hum and easily skipped. But others are thought-provoking, goofy, tawdry, disgusting and downright sexy.

"If," for example, goes one of the questions, "you could henceforth have only one single art form, what do you think it would be?" "If you had to name the single most important quality of a good mate, what would it be?" And then, "If you had to keep one part of your mate's body permanently in the freezer, what part would you save?" Some of the questions need, of course, to be side-stepped if grandmothers or small children are present. But most of them kick animated laughter and table conversation into high gear.

The idea of table questions is that it promotes the possibility of everyone being involved in the discussion. Often, with 8-12 people around the table, the conversation can get segmented with two or three people chatting together here and there, but not engaging with anyone else. Table questions often - not always - remedy that. Table questions get most everyone - except the die-hard recluse or the recently novocained dental patient -- (and that, itself, can be fun) -- involved.

There are also easy, non-competitive table games like "Choice." In the game of "Choice," the person who starts, says two contrasting words, like "Salt or pepper." Then, the person to his or her left chooses one or other. She might say, "Salt." She might say, "pepper." It doesn't matter. No explanation. And certainly no time spent thinking. It's got to be fast. Impulsive. Spontaneous. All around the table. No judgement, no rationalization. Then, very quickly, the one next to the starting person offers two more choices. Maybe

- "Black or white,"
- "Rolling Stones or Jimmy Buffet,"
- "1962 or 1843,"
- "Bicycles or skateboards,"
- "Ice cream or peach pie,"
- "Ernest Hemmingway or Aldous Huxley,"
- "Big breasts or small breasts,"
- "Japanese or Chinese"
- "Facebook or Twitter,"

and on and on...

There is no point to be made, no fact to be proved. Nothing is right or wrong. The goal is simply to generate some laughs and stimulate some quick thinking. And it works! Usually.

Dinners are a fantastic way to build community – to give value to each person present and to offer non-threatening ways to connect and bond with other people. Dinners enhance Dinner enhanced community. Community is the basis of sharing. Community is the core of cooperation.

CELEBRATIONS AND ACKNOWLEDGEMENTS

Everyone – make that everyone – except perhaps a few masochistic mope-heads – appreciates affirmation. Positive words. Compliments. Compliments. Support and approval. Everyone likes to know that they are liked and wanted in this world. That's what birthdays are all about. Or anniversaries. Or weddings. Or even funerals, (though the guest of honor is usually not totally present.) Kind thoughts. Tender sentiments. Saying a resounding, "Yes" to another human.

When someone runs a marathon they deserve a pat on the back. Unless, of course, they babble on and on about it for the next year. In that case, they deserve a slap on the face.

When someone gets a job promotion or graduates from school or makes the Dean's list or even passes organic chemistry ("D" is for "diploma" I used to remind my parents) – when anyone achieves a goal, it's a good thing to recognize that achievement. Whether it's lifting a glass, doing a dance, having a dinner, or simply getting some friends together to give it a big "Hubba-Hubba," applauding good things builds community.

That is what celebrations are all about. You can celebrate Christmas or Easter or Passover. You can celebrate Ramadan or the 4th of July. You can celebrate Thanksgiving or Valentine's Day or Earth Day. But when you celebrate an individual for who they are or what they have accomplished – even if it's just riding the earth around the sun for 365 days – you are acknowledging that he or she is kicking some life butt. He or she is on the field, playing the game and doing it well.

Everyone needs to hear every now and then that they are not just a cog in the wheel. Not just a blip on the screen. Everyone – whether they acknowledge it or not -- likes to be acknowledged as someone special. Likes to feel a pat on the back and hear, "Atta Boy!" "Atta Girl!" And when you hear that from your community – from the people who know you well – it does three things:

1. It builds up the individual.
2. It builds up the community.
3. Makes everyone feel better.

Q. Do you know what George Washington,
Abraham Lincoln and Jesus have in common?
A. They were all born on holidays.

At Hanger Hall, we celebrate birthdays however we can. Sometimes, it works out to have a dinner. Sometimes, we pop a bottle of champagne. Often we have cake. Or ice cream. Or ice cream cake. Or a birthday breakfast. And, if everyone's too busy and there's no time, we at least sing a round of "Happy Birthday" and do a bunch of hugging. The important thing is to honor the person – to enable them to feel appreciated and loved. And just doing that boosts the birthdayee and strengthens the community.

Likewise, when someone's going through a hard time, be it a family or pet death, sickness, loss of a job or a relationship going down the tubes, there are always listening ears at The Hall. Always hugs. Always words of support. That kind of compassion inevitably works to enhance life for all concerned. Celebrating and acknowledging any aspect of another person's life; acknowledging their value in the world or simply offering a kind word are like pebbles dropped in the pond of the day and cause ripples to undulate their goodness throughout each life and into the world far beyond anything you could have imagined. And when it's done in community, the ripples run back and forth for days.

GREETINGS

Google "Greeting Customers." Just do it. Great Googly Moogly! You'll be googly-eyed with the hundreds of sites discussing, teaching, promoting, supporting and sponsoring the value of greeting customers in your store or restaurant or on the phone. Over and over, the message comes through loud and clear that a proper customer greeting inevitably boosts sales and gets people coming back.

You know how it feels to walk in a store and have a clerk or cashier welcome you. You know they've been told to do that by their bosses; but it still feels good. It gives you the feeling that you are more important than whatever paper-work, money-counting, re-stocking, trash-emptying, inventorying, food serving, table-bussing or whatever they were doing. A simple greeting, these googled sites will tell you, makes the customer feel welcome, at home and accepted. And it's absolutely true.

Many of the Greeting sites suggest specific ways of salutation that have proven to be more effective. One site lists these measures of a good welcoming:

1. Have a positive attitude.
2. Greet with their name, if possible.
3. Keep the focus on the customer – not on self.
4. Smile. Keep smiling.
5. Make steady eye contact.

You know the five second rule when your pizza hits the floor? The same is true for greeting customers, says one site. You have five seconds to make a good first impression. And that impression often determines how the rest of the encounter will go.

The same is true in shared housing.

> *People like to be greeted. By name. With a positive attitude. With the focus on them. Smiling and maintaining eye contact. It can make all the difference in that person's day.*

So, you walk into the community kitchen to get some coffee before work. Two others who live with you in that house are there. One is reading the paper, the other on her computer. Both just starting their coffee or tea. Now, keeping in mind that a state of pre-caffeination is a quiet state. A quiet semi-conscious state. A state that does not like loud noises or loud talking or loud banging of pans. Pre-caffeination doesn't like loud at all. It's not a state in which polkas, sirens, bullhorns, firecrackers or trumpeting elk, for example, are welcome.

But... you can still greet the other kitchen day-starters quietly. By name. With a positive attitude. And even with a pre-caffeinated smile.

At Hanger Hall, we regularly greet each other as we walk from room to room, up the stairs, in or out the door. Nothing elaborate. Just a name. Maybe a brief and honest compliment. Maybe a hug. Maybe a smile and a wish for a good time. Or the basic, "Wassup?" So many ways to greet; so little time. But it makes all the difference. The most effortless and uncomplicated greeting can brighten a day, fill a heart, trigger a smile. And, it is one of the easiest and most effective ways of building and maintaining community.

Just now, in my writing, I took a break and went out to the kitchen for a snack. Three housemates were in the kitchen chatting. I said, "Wha's happenin'?"

One of them answered, "We're just lovin' on Megan." Megan laughed.

I asked, "Can I do a little Megan lovin'?"

She answered, "Sure. I love lovin'." I hugged her, got my snack and went back to work. And I'm pretty sure we each went our ways feeling good.

KINDNESS, LIGHTNESS AND LAUGHTER

Q. Why can angels fly?

A. Because they take themselves so lightly.

I think it was jazz artist Maynard Ferguson who said, "Music is far too important for me to take it seriously." But serious is the way we tend to take most of our lives. We are serious about our jobs. Serious about our relationships. Serious about what kind of car we drive. Serious about our brand of toilet paper. Serious about looking good in that new Speedo at the company picnic.

There are, of course, a plethora of things to be taken seriously. It's hard to get a good chuckle - much less a belly laugh - when it comes to say, cancer, Alzheimer's, global warming, terrorism, racism, sexism, starvation, refugees. Just watch CNN or read the news. There's no shortage of horrors that can put the kibosh on mirth in any form.

But when we confuse "serious" and "important" in day-to-day living, we pull the plug on any pool of happiness which is sloshing around waiting to be enjoyed. Cars, jobs, relationships and toilet paper are important - especially toilet paper, depending upon the bean burrito intake; but when we take our cars, jobs relationships, toilet paper or any other part of our foray into the day with nary a titter, sniggle or snort, we rob ourselves of a golden opportunity to bask in the light of lightness and splash in the champagne surf of bliss.

Most of us might agree that kindness, for example, is not just important in life but vital. Fundamental. Necessary. Think of kindness as a balloon. A party balloon floating about, inviting each and every party participant to dance, to laugh, to enjoy each other. But taking the gift of kindness too seriously, pops the balloon. Releases the helium. Loses the magic. And you're left with little stretchy colorful fragments on the floor about which to ponder, to philosophize, or worse yet... as the inspiration for long boring sermons. Like Maynard Ferguson and his music, the grace-filled gift of kindness is far too important to be taken seriously.

And if kindness is important in anyone's daily life, its importance skyrockets when it comes to living in community - in shared, cooperative living. The kindness balloon is all about joy. About delight. About going to 'de light'. Any act of kindness invites gaiety, jollity and joviality. It just feels good. Kindness opens the door to laughter without a punch line or pratfall. It elicits smiles without ever seeing a rainbow, kissing a sleeping child, or smelling fresh coffee and bacon in the morning. Kindness begets smiles and smiles give birth to kindness.

"Be kind," wrote Plato, "for everyone you meet is likely fighting a harder battle," and when you're living in close proximity to other people, the battles that each are fighting individually can sometimes erupt into intrapersonal battles.

Let's say John just had a late-night telephone fight with his girlfriend. He wakes up the next morning groggy, still angry and a bit depressed, heads to the kitchen for some coffee and encounters Jill, one of his housemates. Unbeknownst to John, Jill, just an hour ago got a text from her father saying that her mother had been diagnosed with cancer.

Jill's back is to John. She doesn't see him. She is tense, crying and hovering over the coffee pot. "Excuse me, but others would like a little coffee too," John says with a groggy but hard edge to his voice. These are the first words he's uttered since he hung up with his angry girlfriend and his own fury has not abated. Right now, he's pissed at anything with ovaries.

"Oh, I'm sorry," Jill responds. "But I'm having a hard time and you don't have to be so pushy."

"Well," he replies, "welcome to the hard times party." He fills his cup and leaves the room like a lightning storm on steroids.

"To hell with you!" Jill shouts and immediately launches into a Niagara of tears and snot. Not a great way to start the day.

Situations like this happen in the happiest of homes. Any kind of home. In any traditional nuclear family, things can go nuclear. And in shared housing, where you are not as familiar with each other as brothers, sisters, and parents, things can erupt faster than you can say Pompeii. But the tiniest shred of kindness or the most minuscule molecule of lightness could have defused the morning caffeine debacle.

The modest and unassuming little question, "You OK?" can sometimes work miracles. John didn't know Jill was crying. Jill was clueless that John was pissed. But, as soon as one or the other realized that happiness had left the building, a simple "You OK?" could, at the very least, slowed the storm and opened the door to what they both needed; a little kindness and lightness. Early morning hugs can warm the heart in ways Starbucks would kill for. Then again, getting a blast of another person's morning mouth just might temper the joy.

Kindness and lightness won't grease all the friction. Jill's belly will still be churning with anxiety and John's panties, well-wadded, even if the "You OK?" question and a shared morning-mouth hug were applied. But the potential for future eruptions in the community will almost certainly be ameliorated, because kindness and lightness have the ineffable ability to ripple through a household, rearranging the emotional furniture with such feng shui that fresh air can flow through and everyone ends up breathing better.

Rule of thumb: Always keep kindness and lightness in the wings, ready to go on stage at any moment.

OPEN COMMUNICATION

Over and over again, there's a question that pops up from folks who see and admire the way we operate at The Hall. The question is: Do you have group meetings? And the answer is a resounding, "NO." Many shared housing communities do use and advocate regular group meetings to make decisions, share feelings, focus on direction and so on. And I say, if it works for them, go for it.

My experience with group meetings is that they often turn into a bitch fest. Gripe party.

- "Someone keeps leaving beard or nose hair in the sink. Yuk!"
- "There's rotten food in the fridge and it's not mine."
- "Am I the only one who knows how to use a broom?"
- "Who the hell was playing Grateful Dead this morning at 2:00 a.m.?"
- "Why are there 15 bottles of shampoo in the shower and only 4 of us use it?"
- "When are we going to get some A/C for the kitchen? It's roasting in there."
- "Does no one here know how to remove your hairball from the bathtub drain?"
- "Somebody's cat peed in my guitar case."

...and so on.

Our experience at The Hall is that if the community is well-oiled and engaged on a daily basis, communication happens easily and openly with nary a formal meeting or big hoo-hah. Meetings are what must happen when good communication isn't happening on a regular basis. And when hot issues like the above sit around waiting for a meeting to happen they tend to really heat up and roil and boil and fester. And that's a problem.

According to some extremely well-organized individuals I have met, the secret of a clean desk, for example, is not in just having a cluttered drawer (though that does work), but in dealing -- if at all possible -- with whatever presents itself *when it presents itself*. You pick up a letter or a hard-copy memo which requires a response. Rather than putting it down with a mumbled, "I can get to that later," it's best, say these organizational gurus, to deal with it right then. Immediately. Straight away. At once. Without delay.

That's what we strive to do at The Hall. If there is beard or nose hair in the sink - OK, time for a well-placed "Yuck" or "Eeeeeewww" - then it's best to bring it up whenever the potentially offending person (look for someone with a trimmed beard and nothing hanging out of his nose) shows up. Simply saying something casual like, "Any idea who could be leaving beard and nose hair in the sink?", can defuse a potentially confrontational or gossipy situation which characteristically will escalate into hard feelings and ugly words.

Now, if the response from the well-trimmed and non-furry noser is, "No, but I have groomed my gerbil over the sink a few times," then you....well, you deal with it.

Our experience - and we've had a lot of it - is that kind and direct communication almost always works. Almost. People usually feel respected when they are confronted honestly and gently and maybe even with a little humor. Lightness in communication brings lightness to life anywhere it happens.

So, whether you find wine corks floating in the toilet just as you're sitting down or sufficient cat hair in the corners to knit a tent or a sink filled with baked-on lasagna dishes which look as if they came from an archaeological dig or the new toilet paper roll which has the end dangling under the roll instead of over-the-top like God intended... no matter what the issue, the problem-solving key we have found is open, direct and compassionate communication ASAP.

Then, if you still have meetings, the bitching and griping will mostly have been nipped in the bud.

My time at Hanger Hall was transformative for me.
The first 3 years I lived in a cozy room in the basement.
There were three large windows
with wide sills that opened at ground level
to a bank of mosquito-ridden English ivy and a hickory tree.

I was an introvert from a hilly rural part of Maryland
and a gay artist healing from a very conservative Christian upbringing
that neither accepted my sexuality or saw music as a valid pursuit.
My situation in the basement of Hanger Hall
could not have been better for healing and growing
into the person that I wanted to be. T
he room offered reprieve and quiet safety
and the large house above and beside me
offered a vibrant affirming community.

I could write a whole novel about my colorful experience
with all of the dear and beautiful people who lived there
and how much all of them taught me without meaning to.
As I would sleep at night in that basement room
with the street light making leaf shadows on my floor
and when the others had gone to their rooms too
and all was quiet,
I felt as though we were all on a big sweet boat
that was holding us afloat,
bobbing gently
on an ocean
and i was resting in the belly of that ship.
Alex Krug, 2008-2015

CHAPTER 4

KEEPING IT AFFORDABLE

When it comes to homes, one of the reasons buyers buy is so they can build up equity. When it comes to homes, one of the reasons renters rent is so they don't have to keep up the place and can save and invest in other things. Either way, money is always a huge factor in determining where and how you live.

Every home has built-in-guaranteed-cast iron-fail-safe-no-escaping expenses of taxes, insurance, maintenance, supplies and usually a hefty mortgage. Homeowners are liable for every penny on that expense account. Renters are liable for a portion of it. Co-operative living offers unique advantages in the money department. When you share a house, you share expenses in almost every regard. That usually means everyone pays less than the average renter and a whole lot less than the homeowner. For example:

SHARED UTILITIES

Whether you own or rent, you probably have a fridge. That fridge is going to use electricity no matter what. If you're the renter or owner, you pay for every amp, volt and ohm. But, if there are three or four using the same fridge, the bill gets split 3-4 ways. Everybody saves.

Whether you own or rent, you will hopefully have heat and maybe A/C not just for your bedroom, but for your dining room, kitchen, and living room. As a renter, you will pay for that heat and air. 3-4 people sharing dining room, kitchen, and living room means the bill gets split 3-4 ways. Everybody saves.

Porch lights. Security lights. Kitchen, bathroom, living room lights, internet, cable... shared means savings. Got a hot-tub? Gonna cost you some bucks to heat, clean and fill that little joy wagon. 3-4 folks living together split that cost. And hot-tubs are always more fun with more people. With or without the swim suits. No. Actually, without is more fun.

Sharing utilities helps keep it affordable. At Hanger Hall, the electric and gas bill is shared by all. Average monthly bill is around $60/per person. I, the owner, pay the water, cable and internet bills. In our area of the country, the average utility bill (electric, heating, water, garbage) (not including internet or cable) is $152/month/household. Sharing saves.

And, when it comes to saving, never overlook energy-efficient (read "money saving") appliances. If your kitchen has a fifteen year-old refrigerator, chances are you could replace it with a brand new energy-saving model that could pay for itself in a few years. And it would look spiffy as well. Spiffy is important. Even with refrigerators. Likewise with heating and A/C. If your units are old, chances are they are draining your wallet far more than a shiny new one which can offer the same heat and cooling at a fraction of the cost.

BUYING IN BULK

When there are 6-8 people living together and sharing the same kitchen, it makes little sense to have 6-8 bags of potatoes, 6-8 bags of onions, 6-8 bags of sugar, 6-8 sets of spices, 6-8 cans of Comet, dishwashing liquid, washing detergent, window cleaner, etc. Buying in bulk inevitably is cheaper than standard retail. You can get 50 pounds of potatoes at the local farmer's market, for maybe $8-10. Onions and garlic, likewise. Then you have the mega-box-wholesale-club stores which sell cases of cleaning goods and everything else, at a fraction of grocery store prices.

In our area we have CSA–Community Supported Agriculture–with which you pay a regular weekly/monthly fee; and local farms fill a box of locally grown, fresh produce (sometimes meat) for you each week. If you order a weekly box, there is often more than you can eat or sometimes things you wouldn't eat even if the only other option were Spam. But, with several others living with you, the cost of the box could be split and someone would gladly share the feast and even eat the gag-inducing whatever. Sharing saves.

LEASE vs. RENT

At Hanger Hall, we have never, ever used a standard lease or rental agreement form (available at Staples, Office Depot and all over Google.) But some folks think it wise and in some cases, it could be useful. Over 40+ years, we have had only one minor legalese sna-fu in which a rental/lease agreement might... make that "MIGHT" have been helpful. It finally has to do with how legalistically or how lightly we take ourselves. (See Chapter 3.)

But, when it comes to lease and/or rental, it finally comes

around to tenant mindset and what works. There are some tenants in shared housing who want a guarantee that they will have a legal place in the home for at least 6 months or more. There are some tenants who would rather be loose, fluid and ready to jump ship at a moment's notice. To my mind, neither is desirable in a shared housing situation.

The two most compelling qualities in a happy and satisfied shared housing tenant are 1) Flexibility and 2) Groundedness.

Unless your shared housing situation is built on a kind of B&B, revolving door, in-and-out platform, you will want some kind of basic understanding of commitment to the community. A home where people cometh and goeth at a whim doth not beget groundedness or community. Likewise, where people are required to commit to 6 months or a year at a time doth not beget flexibility. There must be -- as the Tao Te Ching might say -- balance.

We have found a 30-day notice to be a happily working arrangement. When a newbie moves in, part of the understanding (never in print, only in conversation, handshakes and hugs) is that either the landlord (me) (Benevolent Dictator) or the newbie, must give 30 days notice before they leave – or are asked to leave.

In the 40+ year history of Hanger Hall Living Cooperative, with hundreds having lived here, less than a half dozen have been asked to leave. The 30-day notice offers grounding and flexibility. The handshake-hug-non-paper-work agreement offers trust, and a sense of trust on which every successful shared housing community thrives.

We were a strange family of very different people
who supported each other,
laughed together
and cried together.
If you haven't been to a Hanger Hall party,
then you've never been to a party!
It will always have a reserved spot in my heart.

Natalie Hewitt, 2010 – 2012

I moved to Hanger Hall
shortly after moving to Asheville.
My time there
provided the much-needed community
that I was sorely needing.
The end of my stint at the Hall
was marked by challenges
with other community members,
but that does not negate the fact
that this place served me generously.
Those struggles solely exemplify
that living with a large group of people
has its ups and downs.

Craig Deutsch, 2015 – 2017

CHAPTER 5

THE STRUCTURE

For 30+ years, I traveled with my band, The Jazz Fantasy. We didn't play that much straight-up jazz but led an excellent fantasy life. We played hundreds of college campuses, churches, festivals and elementary schools in this country. Then, with the DOD Showcase Tours we traveled to 26 countries over a 12-year period. That's right! The U.S. Defense Department spent your tax dollars toting a group of 7 goofy musicians and dancers around the world to make music. Five or six shows a week. Didn't make us a great living; but it did make for a great life.

As any musician knows, however, it's all about the sound. If the sound ain't right, gonna be a bad night. And one of the main determining factors of the sound is the room. You can have the finest musicians playing the finest instruments through the finest sound system; but if the room has crappy acoustics, it's going to sound like ...crap. When it comes to sound, to ambience, to communication, the room always wins. Always.

And so it is with the building that is used for shared community housing. You can have a house full of the nicest people, a fine organization, an excellent understanding of the group's M.O.; but the building can take it down. Jimmy Buffett's metaphor of oysters and pearls is ever so apt when it comes to structures for housing. Most exist as oysters, but some become pearls. Here are a few ways to encourage the pearly process in a shared-living home.

COMMON SPACE/PRIVATE SPACE – THE BALANCE

One of the prime problems of living in community is... you're living in community. You've got people around much of the time. The same damn people. Over and over, day after day. And sometimes, you just want to be alone. No matter how much you love them; there are times when you don't want to be around them. Honeybees in a hive don't seem to mind. Thousands of maggots in your garbage can appear to love it. But most humans want a little get-away time and space built in to their daily lives. Privacy is absolutely necessary.

Paper-thin walls through which you can hear snores, farts, and love-making will not work for long in community housing. Cheap hollow doors with huge gaps under or around will not work. You can put up curtains to keep the neighbors from watching you perform your nightly Naked-Dirty-Dancing Zumba Routine, but with wimpy walls and dismal doors, your housemates will hear not only the music, but also your own grunts, groans and squeals. And if there's someone in your house who enjoys hearing that you don't want them in your house. You just don't.

Along with privacy, however, people need places to stretch their minds, their bodies, their spirits - places that offer more things to look at than their pile of laundry - more things to contemplate than their unmade bed and empty pizza boxes - more places to sit than the only-a-bit-torn flamingo-pink upholstered vanity chair you found at Goodwill ten years ago for $2. That's what common space is all about. Common space is everyone's space – a place to chat it up and giggle a bit with your housemates and guests. It can be the kitchen, the living room, dining room, hallway, front porch or back deck. At Hanger Hall, being a large Victorian mansion, some of our common areas include the laundry room, hot-tub room, swimming pool area, upper and lower solariums. A Grand Hall and several sitting and dining areas. That's right! Hot-tub and pool. We have discovered that creature comforts make everyone more comfortable.

What makes a common area a good common area? Here are a few ideas:

1. Cleanliness
2. No personal stuff lying around
3. Inviting
4. Comfortable seats
5. Good lighting—NON NEON—easy on the eyes, with lamps for reading
6. Good feng shui
7. Objects d'art
8. A small Bluetooth or computer-compatible sound system
9. Maybe a TV -- Maybe*
10. WiFi

*TVs can be great for entertainment, but they can be bullies. They can dominate a common area, inhibiting conversation and requiring anyone in the common area to either watch or leave the room.

A shared home with truly private spaces and welcoming, uncluttered and clean common areas has an enormous advantage over homes which don't.
Life simply goes more smoothly with that combo.

BATHROOMS

Rule #1: You gotta have 'em.

Rule #2: You gotta keep 'em clean.

Whoever is in charge (See Chapter 7) must... make that MUST make sure that everything in the bathroom is always... make that ALWAYS in working order. Keep a plunger beside every toilet. A plumber's friend is everyone's friend. Also, it's a good idea to always have a professional plumber whom you trust, one who is prompt and who won't eat your VISA card. Promptness is what makes a good plumber great.

One excellent idea is to ask this trusted plumber if he or she will offer a good deal if you promise to call them and only them for your plumbing issues. It usually works. In any event, having the name and phone number of a plumber posted somewhere in the house is an excellent... make that EXCELLENT idea.

And how, I say, how do you keep 'em clean? Ideas:

1. Hire someone and add the cost to the rent.
2. Constantly encourage cleanliness.
3. Pray for a bathroom fairy.
4. Slap the shit (so to speak) out of anyone who leaves it dirty.

OK, 3 & 4 are not always workable. But 1&2 are. Many folks will gladly kick in a few bucks a month to know that there won't be beard, nose or gerbil hair (See Chapter 3) where you brush your teeth, nor a hairball the size of Montana in the shower drain, nor a pile of towels which smell as if they have been hanging in the Roquefort caves of France.

Likewise, unless your home population is light on the Neatniks and heavy on the Slobs (See Chapter 2), many times, simple humorous suggestions here and there work for many to be reminded of cleaning up after themselves and maybe a little extra.

KITCHEN

When it comes to the importance of clean common areas, Zee Kitchen Trumps All. The prime attribute of any kitchen – other than being a gathering place – is providing things for you to put in your mouth. Yes, IN YOUR MOUTH. And not only to put in your mouth, but then to chew, swallow and digest. It doesn't get much more personal and intimate than that. A kitchen is where you gather things to put into your body. And even the most primitive hunter/gatherer would know that when you put dirty things into your body, the results will not get you laughing.

So, just the sight of a dirty kitchen can kill an appetite for many. And dirty food out of a dirty kitchen can kill you. When city health inspectors come to check out a restaurant, they don't check out the coat racks, the chairs, the art, placemats. No! They check out the kitchen. Restaurants with dirty kitchens get the kibosh. And for good reason.

Indeed, kitchens are gathering spots in most homes. And that includes shared homes. Kitchens are the hub. You can have the most swanky living room, the most comfortable den, an inviting back deck; but most folks will still head for the kitchen first, and often, last. More of a reason to keep it clean.

At Hanger Hall, we have a Kitchen Fairy. We do, indeed. And that would be me. As it happens, I truly enjoy cleaning the kitchen.

Truly. Nor am I a practicing masochist in any other regard. At The Hall, our MO is that no one leaves dirty dishes, pots or pans. But there is always a sink to scrub, counters to wipe down, a microwave to clean out, a floor to sweep and/or mop. There is a dishwasher to run and empty. It takes about 30-40 minutes each morning for me to make the kitchen spotless; and has become a kind of meditation for me. Win-Win!

A hotel manager once told me that the rule of thumb for their house-cleaning staff was to clean each room in such a way that it looks as if it had never been lived in before. That is the goal of The Kitchen Fairy: to make each resident feel, upon entering the kitchen, that they are the first ones ever to eat there. And that, Lil' Buckaroos, is one fine way to start any day. Keep 'dem kitchens clean!

Now, if your house does not have a Kitchen Fairy who gets great pleasure from fairying, one option would be to hire a kitchen fairy who gets part of his or her rent deducted for flitting about early in the day or late at night; flitting about with a rag in one hand and a bottle of cleaner in the other. Fairies are sometimes closer than you think.

APPLIANCES

Refrigerators, freezers, ovens, cook-tops, microwaves, toasters, coffee-makers, coffee-grinders, dishwashers, disposals, compactors... they all add to a positive kitchen experience. And, they all cost money. Lots of money. And sooner or later, they all break down. And when they break down, they again cost money. Often, lots of money.

In the beginning was the word, and the word was Maintenance Agreements. At least for the big stuff. Toaster, coffee-makers, coffee grinders, blenders, all the little yada yada... no problem. Cheap and easy to replace. But, the big boys – the kind that cost $1000 or more

– get a maintenance agreement. Shared-living appliances get a lot more use than the average and, therefore, require more TLC. At Hanger Hall, good maintenance agreements have saved our butts again and again. If the fridge goes down in the middle of the night, there could be a heap of food going down the drain. Ching-ching. And then you gotta get that chill box back on line. Ching-ching. Maintenance agreements can ease the pain of the ching-ching. If your appliances are old with no agreement, not to fear. Well, maybe a little fear. But when they heave their last hurrah, go for a new one WITH a maintenance agreement.

Not only does a shared housing kitchen need to be clean, it needs to be efficient. (See Chapter 4) Always, always, always check the energy rating for any major gas or electric driven appliance. Super-efficient appliances not only save everyone money, but they are a small step toward keeping Miami and The Florida Keys above water.

SOUNDPROOFING

One of the downsides of cooperative living is the sometimes crowded feeling you get. Even if you have plenty of common area, when everyone is there and active in some way, it can feel claustrophobic.

Let's just say that during the night there was a huge snowstorm. Big drifts. Unplowed street. Even Shel Silverstein couldn't tell where the sidewalk ends. One by one, the groggy residents stumble out for coffee and phone calls announcing school and work cancellations. After the initial ooohs, aaahs, and appreciation expressed that the power's still on... after resident Wild-Man Jim runs out front in his skivvies to make a snow angel and dares everyone else to do the same... after the three boy and girlfriend guests do the walk of shame to the bathroom... after everyone has played on their phones and after the snow begins coming down again... it begins to settle in that all are stuck in this one house for at least a day. Enter Cabin Fever. Enter Cabin Fever on steroids.

Board games can help. TV movies can help. Books can help. Phones can help. But one real way to cut down on that stuck-in-an-elevator sensation is something, unfortunately, can't be done in an instant. It's called soundproofing and it works wonders. Rugs, carpets, curtains, big sofas, cushioned chairs, pillows, tapestries, dropped ceiling tile... anything that absorbs sound and doesn't reflect it can actually give your common areas a feeling of expansiveness.

We all know about sound pollution in urban situations but it's real in the home as well. Whether it be footsteps, dropped cooking pans, telephone conversations, any conversation, click of computer keyboards, strumming of a guitar, laughter, moans, groans, a sneeze, fart, or belch...anything that humans do intentionally or unintentionally to make sound can create a feeling of crowdedness.

Now, if you're having a party, sound is what you want. Lots of sound. Any party-thrower worth her big balloons knows that happy sound pollution (music, laughter, conversation) is essential to any happening party. And one of the reasons party bands start soft and gradually play louder is so that the conversation will get loud and the cacophony (along with the booze) will create that party atmosphere. But, unless your shared living house is a 24/7 Party-Till-You-Drop kind of place, soundproofing will be a blessing. Good soundproofing actually makes your space feel much larger than it really is.

That, of course, takes time and money. But both time and money are always well-spent in making your shared home more ear-friendly.

PARKING

One of the bug-a-boos in shared housing is that everyone usually has a car and some have more than one. In the standard family home, the parent or parents might have a car but younger kids...not so much. Multiple parking places are not usually found in "normal" housing. Apartments or condos may have one or two spaces. But if you have three or four living together, whatchagonna do?

Enter those words which we have each said or thought about one thing or another throughout our lives: Why didn't we think of that? Before you even get started in cooperative living, check the parking. And if there isn't enough for residents and a guest or two, find another place or make friends with a neighbor who's got an extra space or three.

SECURITY

Everyone wants some degree of security. Even the most live-for-the-moment-love-the-one-you're-with-starry-eyed-peace-on-earth-let's-all-just-love-each-other free spirit wants to feel that his or her belongings won't mysteriously get damaged or disappear. The bad news is there is nothing you can do to guarantee that won't happen. The good news is that living in community tends to dissuade would-be thieves. Locks on individual doors might be helpful as long as someone knows where a key to each room is kept. No one likes, for example to smell smoke in the house and not be able to get into every room to check it out.

According to many security articles on the internet (it's got to be true, right?), light is the biggest deterrent to criminal activity. At Hanger Hall, we leave low-wattage lights on in all the common areas and over more than four decades, have had (knock on wood) nothing stolen from the house. Also, when you live in a house where people come and go at odd hours, no self-respecting thief is going to take the chance of walking into a well-lit and constantly inhabited space.

Dogs work as security for some people. The only problem we have found with dogs is that most canines are usually not clever enough to discern the bad guys from the good. We had a dog that, by his actions, seemed to be sure that the pizza delivery guy was a terrorist. And we were pretty sure if the dog ever met a truly bad guy he would wag and beg for a treat. But, many single women I have known swear that having a dog–even a pizza-guy killer–makes them feel safer at home and/or out on a walk.

Mostly, it's common sense:

- If you have a kick-ass sound system in your front room visible through the window on a busy street, having curtains on that window is probably not the worst idea. It may pay to advertise, but this kind of ad can cost you.
- Anyone who parks his/her car outside without locking the car is...well...stupid.
- Leaving cash lying around out in the open is a great way to lead someone into temptation.
- Leaving a phone, iPad, or computer unaccompanied on the front porch or back deck makes you an official member of the 40-watt club.
- When your house has a big party with lots of friends and friends of friends, it's not a bad idea for some resident of the house to stay semi-sober and at least partially alert.
- If a resident is leaving town for a while and the room will be unoccupied, be sure everyone knows so the room can be even casually, but regularly monitored.

Here's the thing: most people are honest. And honest people attract honest people. But some people do steal and some people do trash others' possessions and some people do hurt other people. Rule of thumb at Hanger Hall: Be trusting. And be smart.

A "I had to get rid of my dog to move in here".
Suzanne's matter-of-fact-toned statement caught me a little off guard
as I was making an egg sandwich
in the Jimmy Buffet inspired community kitchen.

"I'm glad you're here and I like your dog but I wanted you to know
that it doesn't feel fair. I mean, I understand that you're
the owner's partner and all,
but still…I just needed to get that off my chest",
she said with a sigh of relief followed by a smile.

I lived romantically with Howard for 6 years
and soon realized the other side of being the partner
of the head of the house.
Yes, there were special privileges…
and sometimes they had social consequences
with other members of the house.

Fortunately, in most instances all parties involved
had the maturity and communication skills to honor each other
and move through peacefully.

A sanctuary to be thy self,
unchained from the neediness of conventionality,
Hanger Hall shows you the benefits
of living outside of the 'norm'.

The practice of living unconventionally has its benefits.
It releases you from the concepts of

what you should be
and allows you to be who you are,
to love who you love.

Living in a diverse community
where the foundation is co-operation,
which inevitably leads us to a need to accept others
even when we don't agree or understand,
can have profound impacts on
how we see ourselves
and the world around us.
What if we could be who we want
and still be accepted?
Love who we love
and still be respected?
Share our past,
our dreams,
our fears,
our insecurities
and still be greeted in the morning with kindness and compassion.
This doesn't mean you can slack on your dishes
or continue to have loud guests after 10 pm,
but it does mean you can explore your authentic self,
however quirky it may be
and still be part of the community
– as long as you do your dishes.

T'was a magical time in my life.
While my family and friends would often tell me
I was 'living in a fantasy world'
I would reply with an,
"exactly, and that is the way I like it."

Hayley Joyell Smith, 2010 – 2016

CHAPTER 6

MAKING THE HOUSE A HOME

A house keeps the rain off your head. A house keeps you warm in the winter. A house is a place to change your underwear. A house offers a place to sleep, eat and poop. A home, however, is where your heart is happy. And in a house with several people in residence the more happy hearts—the better. That's what homes are all about.

Even the most bland and boring house can be made into a welcoming, gracious, fun and exciting home. We say, "I want to go home." We don't say, "I want to go to a house." Home is where the heart is; house has no heart. "A house is not a home," wrote Ben Franklin, "unless it contains food and fire for the mind as well as body." So, if you're in the market for a place for hearts to gather, you gotta make 'dat house a home. Here are some ways that have worked for us.

DECORATING

Call it cliché, call it oversimplification, call it chauvinism, sexism, bigotry or whatever you want; but from my experience, most women and nearly all gay men are better at décor – for body or home – than almost any hetero man. As a hetero, I had a girlfriend who, when she would take me shopping, would step out of the dressing room in a new frock and say, "Give me Gay Howard." So, if you're needing to upgrade the look of your home, gathering your women and gay friends over for a party is not at all a bad idea.

You can decorate with art or with chairs, tables and sofas. You can decorate with rugs and lamps and shelves of books. You can decorate with photos. At Hanger Hall, we have a large shelf with a picture of each of our Hallians. Each resident chooses and contributes a picture of themselves. You can decorate with plants and cut flowers. You can decorate with ceiling fans and wine racks. You can decorate with rocks and vases and ceramic plates. You can decorate with a child's stuffed animals, with mementos, with coffee-table books, with candles and incense, with stemware and water pitchers. Of course, paint colors are crucial and the names of paints are both hilarious and enchanting. And if you don't like the name of the paint, but like the color, you can always hang a moniker on that puppy. We named the color of my bedroom "Patagonia Nude." Who wouldn't want to sleep there? So many ways to decorate, so little time.

Decorating – however simple and straightforward – truly transforms a room into a living space, more than a place just to come out of the rain, but a place to feel at peace, to feel welcomed, to feel alive, to feel "at home". And one of the most agreeable parts of decorating is that it's fluid. Just because you have that potted bonsai guava tree in one corner does not mean it can't be moved to another room at any time and even every day. Trying out lamps and art and candles in a variety of rooms and settings keeps things interesting and trounces the boredom factor. On the other hand, when you find what feels like the perfect placement for an object, you can ensconce it, bless it and call it good.

Nor does decorating have to be pricey or serious. That's why God made Goodwill and whimsy. Don't ever forget the value of whimsy in your décor. You can drop $15 at a consignment store and come home with a peacock feather lamp or set of Jimmy Buffet pillows or maybe a Buddha made from beer bottle caps that will give your home furnishings a fine bump. Whatever expresses your personality and those of your housemates will work. And if it doesn't, that's why God invented re-gifting.

MUSIC

Two of the main social lubricants in our culture are music and alcohol. They are key ingredients of most weddings, birthday parties, anniversaries, celebrations of any kind; even funerals. I attended a divorce celebration a few years back which involved as much food, booze, music and dancing as any wedding. Music and alcohol - especially together – encourage conversation and laughter, dancing and flirting, bawdy jokes and old tales, hospitality and conviviality – exactly what you want in any party or joyful celebration.

Living in shared housing is not ever a constant party. But a little music playing in the background when you're in the kitchen (see Chapter 3),,living, or dining rooms, almost always greases the social connection of the people there. Not that music has to be going all the time. Quiet for reading, conversation, and meditation is essential. But, if silence is golden, good background music here and there, is at least silver.

Most grocery stores play music for the customers and employees. Most restaurants as well. Music is in the malls, on the streets with buskers, in massage studios, some hotel lobbies, and everywhere in Disney World. Music and human gathering places are definitely intertwined in our world.

In order to be an effective social lubricant, of course, the music must appeal to the present company. A mix of Black Sabbath and Metallica would probably not fly for dinner music in an assisted living facility. Nor would a medley of Barry Manilow's greatest hits stir the social waters of a college party. But there are puuuuuuhlenty of musical options available; and if you know your housemates even moderately well, you will know what will increase the OMGs and diminish the WTFs.

FENG SHUI

It literally means "wind-water." It's a Chinese philosophical system of getting things and people flowing together. In decorating terms, it means arranging the furniture, rugs, lamps, art in such a way that it feels natural – as if you or your guests or wind and water could flow through the room without interference. Humans are, after all, mostly water; and without wind or breath, we are not going to feng much shui.

Nor is Feng Shui just a matter of furniture placement. In conversation, Feng Shui can mean allowing the tête-à-tête to run unimpeded, starting and stopping naturally with laughter and contemplation dancing in and out without any obstacles.

You know you're doing your best feng shui when you feel like you are part of what is happening – part of the flow. OK, if you're feeling a warm flow in your pants, that's something else entirely. Incontinence is not necessarily part of the ancient Chinese teaching.

But one of the primary ways of making a house a home is by being aware of how things flow, be it the way people move through a room, through discussions, or through problem solving. Remember, of course, that you'll never, ever, ever get everything perfectly flowing. Lose that silly notion right now. But, when each person in the house is aware of the need for feng shui, it's amazing what changes can happen.

CREATURE COMFORT

As mentioned in Chapter 5, in one of my former lives, I was a traveling musician. For all of its aura of romance, mystery and intrigue, the life of a traveling musician can actually be immensely challenging. Yes, there are the high times (musically and drug-related), there is the joy of meeting and performing for different people every night, there were the groupies (drummers and guitar players always get the girl...or the boy, as orientation dictates); but there is also the day-after-day being packed in a van or plane often before dawn to travel for hours only to go through the same set-up, sound-check, grab-a-bite, performance, take-down, pack-up, roll a fat one, try to sleep for a bit and be ready to go in the morning. And then, there's the dirty underwear.

Our band stayed together for many years – many more than the average non-super-star bands normally do – and I believe one of the reasons for our longevity was what I call "creature comfort." Creature comfort can be a cushy lounge chair. A decent pillow. It can be a working and quiet A/C in a hotel bedroom. It can be a decent meal at a not-fast-food eatery. It can be a book read aloud during the long rides in the van. It can be a shoulder-rub, foot-rub, head-rub, almost-anything-rub. It can be a shared bottle of good whiskey at the end of the day.

On the road, as leader of the band, I made sure that we had every amenity that the tour could afford and often went over budget just wanting the Creature Comfort (CC) level to ride high. When the low CC light came on, discontent, bitching and complaining and sometimes, out-and-out bad juju, was sure to come.

In a shared housing situation, you can never underestimate the value of creature comfort.

- Decent and comfortable furniture in the living room or conversation areas.
- Lots of pillows. A stack of nice, squishy pillows in a room where people gather can make all the difference in attitudes and way of behaving.
- If you can afford to air-condition the common areas, do it!
- If there's a fireplace, get it working.
- Don't have a decent sound system? Get one.
- Comfy rugs that feel good on bare feet.
- A bottle of wine that can be pulled out and shared for no particular reason.

When your home feels comfortable and inviting, spirits and attitudes inevitably rise.

At Hanger Hall, a big chunk of the rent goes to cover basics (See Chapter 4): potatoes, onions, cleaning goods, toilet paper, etc. One way to make sure the CC low light doesn't start blinking is to keep everything expected in stock, so you never run out of cleaning supplies or laundry detergent or light bulbs or -- God forbid -- toilet paper. A house with many people and no toilet paper is not a happy home. Trust me on this one. And speaking of paper, having a decent newspaper delivered to your door each morning automatically offers a homey atmosphere to the place. We have the New York Times and local paper delivered. Each day's issues tend to stay on the kitchen table and are read by whoever might be eating breakfast or lunch or just chilling.

Do all these things cost money? Hell, yes. Are they worth every penny? Abso - friggin'- lutely. And who is responsible for making sure the house supplies are present and ready to go? Chapter 7, coming up.

Chapter 6

Hanger Hall made it possible for me
to be a musician.
When the overhead was low enough,
there was a possibility
of me spending my time doing what I love.

To keep the mess down in the communal kitchen,
some basic staples
like potatoes and onions
were provided as part of the rent.
Just knowing I would survive
took the pressure off
and gave me room to dream.
The grand staircase and the high ceilings
took away the sting
of not having much money.
I started out in the basement room with no windows,
but I didn't mind because
I spent my time writing in the common rooms
and soon I got lucky and moved up to a room
on the second floor.
After a couple years, the top room opened up
and I slept with a 360° view.

There was often somebody visiting
and some interesting conversation
in the dining room
or the Jacuzzi
downstairs at night.
I loved the company in the kitchen
that kept me from becoming a recluse
in my long writing jags.
I could always come down
and see what conversations were happening,
and join in if I wanted to.

I look back on those years with great gratitude,
and the beautiful house
is still a part of every tour I give to friends who come to visit.

David Wilcox, 1986 – 1991

CHAPTER 7

WHO'S IN CHARGE HERE?

DEMOCRACY AND ALL THAT STUFF

Some co-ops use the democratic process to run the show. More power to them. At Hanger Hall, we tried to be good Americans with one vote/one person. We tried it for several years and it was a disaster. It nearly killed the community.

Ain't nothing wrong with democracy as a concept for Western Civilization. But, no offense Greeks, from our experience for over 4 decades, democracy in co-op living sucks. Trying to make every decision a democratic decision is an excellent way to set yourself up for years of therapy. Even in a democracy, you know, we elect leaders. That's the whole point. Leadership is vital for any human endeavor. Without strong, capable, insightful, efficient and compassionate leadership, any organization is doomed. So, in trying to solve every co-op household problem by voting on it without any strong leadership, you're circling the bowl and going down soon.

Hanger Hall began, however, with the democratic ideal. Our house meetings started out, well...let's just say, "dreadful." And then got worse. Really. Think about it. After a full day of work or school, who wants to sit around and vote on how toilets should be cleaned? Or who's going to get the lawnmower fixed? Or who's been cooking bacon in the veggie-designated frying pan? Or whether Clorox is an eco-friendly cleaning agent? Or why you-know-who can't learn to keep their love-making from sounding like a Tarzan movie?

Finally, after a few years, our house meetings evolved into either jokes or out-and-out bitch sessions. We tried meditation. We tried a moment of silence. We tried passing a joint around before each meeting to soothe the angry beasts or at least get a few wads out of the panties. We tried agreeing to keep the meetings to only a half-hour instead of the two-hour heated marathon discussions we sometimes had over such critical topics like:

- Keeping the toilet plunger near the toilet
- Not leaving heinous-smelling hiking boots in the hall
- Not flushing during showers
- No stashing multiple six-packs of beer in the fridge with no party in sight
- Buying tush-and-hemorrhoid-friendly toilet paper
- Cleaning out the fridge: Is it meat? Is it cake? Is it meat-cake?
- Running the vacuum cleaner at 2:00 in the morning
- Moldzilla in the basement
- ...and on and on.

Don't know who said it first, but, after an interminable number of democratic meetings, someone must have finally expressed what most of us were feeling: **These f****** meetings are a waste of time.**

Chapter 7

THE BAD-ASS BENEVOLENT DICTATOR, AKA BD

I agreed, and from that moment on – may have been a moment, may have been a few months – we smoked a bit in those days – we were a band, after all – I took the reins and made the decisions. I checked on toilet plungers and smegma-smelling boots and toilet paper and posted quiet hours. In short, I became the dictator of Hanger Hall. They called me "benevolent dictator;" but dictator it was. And is. I make and enforce the rules. I choose who lives here and who doesn't. I purchase all the house goods and pay all the house bills. I post notices on our bulletin board and our Facebook page. I buy food for our house dinners and cook it. Everybody cleans up. I am the one in charge when a window breaks or a roof leaks or a heater goes belly up. I make the calls, line up the repairs and pay the tab. It ain't always easy being a Benevolent Dictator (BD), but it certainly streamlines the operation of a co-op and mostly keeps everyone happy. Much more so than the democratic process.

Everyone beside the BD is still responsible for keeping common areas clean and tidy (See Chapter 2), honoring quiet hours, folding laundry when you take it from the dryer no matter whose it is, cleaning out fridges and freezers and being kind. Kindness. That's always a biggie.

One extenuating factor of this Benevolent Dictatorship is that I own the house. I bought the house in 1973 and have been paying the mortgages ever since. Hanger Hall is technically and legally my home. But, there's far more than legality and ownership going on here. There is community. So I make it clear –we all make it clear –to each resident that Hanger Hall is their home. When residents come back from a trip, we always welcome them "home." We encourage traveling house members to call "home" and check in. This is our home. Truly, **our** home. And that is very clear to each and all.

Being home offers a sense of belonging. It's not just a place where you floss your teeth and change your underwear, though both are important. It's a place where each of us is welcomed, accepted, honored, respected. "The ache for home," says Maya Angelou, "lives in all of us, the safe place where we can go as we are and not be questioned." If a shared housing/co-op does not feel like home to every resident, the entire community will suffer. Good leadership enables that to happen.

WHERE DO YOU FIND A GOOD LEADER?

So, how is a leader chosen? In our case, I am the owner of the house and after the debacle of trying to vote on every facet of living together – from roach-condo lasagna dishes tucked under common-area couches to the clogged toilet from a half-roll of toilet paper stuck in the pipes after a night of jalapeno/alligator taco to used condoms in the shower stall, I was, by default, perhaps, selected to lead this wild and unruly group of people as their BD.

There are plenty of other ways leaders can be chosen. You don't have to own the house. Many co-op houses are rented, which means a leader must be chosen by the residents. Back to debilitating democracy. Or, it could be someone who has amassed a following of friends whose trust and confidence are unquestionably with that person. My sense is that there are naturally natural leaders – people who, for one reason or many, have somehow learned how to lead. And, from my experience, most folks recognize that quality in a person and will willingly follow that leader.

Steven Gaskin, the leader who founded The Farm in Summertown, Tennessee (See Chapter 1), had a following of several hundred hippies who had traveled with him all over the U.S. So, when they landed in central Tennessee, he was already their acknowledged leader. No vote necessary. He remained their leader for many years.

Having been the BD for more than four decades, I've gotten into the flow of our community and have helped guide the flow. And a few things have become ever so clear: A good community leader:

- **Leads by example, not by directive.** If you want things kept clean and uncluttered, the leader must do some active cleaning regularly. I clean the kitchen, for example, every morning for about 40 minutes. I hire someone to come in and clean the common areas weekly. I wash the house laundry (we use cloth and not paper towels —an eco thing.), mostly take out the recycling & trash, etc. I shop, cook and prepare meals for the residents 1-3 times each week. If the leader ain't cleaning, ain't nuthin' the leader can say to get the residents doin' it. If the leader ain't constantly focusing on building community, no one can complain if community withers.
- **Stays in close touch with the residents** – is aware to some extent of what they are going through. If the leader sees puffy eyes or tears, it's always wise to ask if there's anything you can do and/or open your arms for a hug if that's what they want. A good leader greets each person whenever and wherever you see them – passing in the hall, in the kitchen, returning from work or school, on the way to the bathroom. And there's nothing like the classic, "How ya doin'?"
- **Does everything possible to keep the house in good shape and the residents well cared for.** If the toilet's clogged, a good leader gets out the plunger or calls Roto-Whiz immediately. If the roof starts leaking, that leader gets his/her sweet self to Home Depot for some of that black goop that never comes out of your clothes or better yet, calls someone who's

good with ladders. A good leader never runs out of toilet paper. Ever. And, if the hot water heater goes out, that puppy needs to get fixed or replaced NOW! When the residents see that their leader is actively and immediately dealing with house problems, the residents feel cared for. And smiles trump grumbles.

BUDGET

One the leader's primary jobs is dealing with the bucks. If your community doesn't have a budget, you're screwed. And it's the leader's job to carve out that budget, maintain that budget and then make sure there's enough rent coming in to pay for it. If you're the leader, you can never, ever - make that never-ever-ever - over-estimate what it takes to operate a house. Sure, you got the mortgage or lease payments and gas and electric and water and cable and internet and appliances and maintenance agreements. Got that covered? But what about the lawn mower repair you didn't expect? Or the circular saw, wood and sheetrock you needed to build that closet? Did someone say "insurance?" Fire? Flood? Liability? What about that new "Rain-simulating" showerhead that everyone wants? Garbage bags? Potatoes, onions, flour, sugar, cleaning goods, half-and-half, butter, coffee? Gotta have 'em. You get the picture.

Allow me, if you will, to repeat myself:

You can never, ever - make that never-ever-ever - over-estimate what it takes to operate a house. Especially a shared house.

So the rent needs to be set accordingly. Low enough to be affordable, high enough to pay the bills. And know beyond the shadow of a doubt that increases in rent are part of the party. It's the leader's job to do all that. Does it call for creativity? Hell, yes. Sometimes, rooms need to be divided up so more people can live there and budget can be met without the rent skyrocketing. Sometimes, bathrooms need to be improved or modified to accommodate multiple poopers. In our town, there's a law that requires one bathroom for every four people living in the same house. It's not only a good law, it's a wise practice. More than 4 to a toilet, sink and shower in any living situation is asking for upset residents and peed pants.

ADMISSION

So, how do you find the right people to move in together? The kind of people you want to live with? Hanger Hall started with my band. We all knew each other and the various boy- and girl-friends who inevitably come with the package. So, when we started our co-op in 1973, we started with an already established community of folks who had been traveling together for several years. Similarly, in a way, as with Steven Gaskin and The Farm. The original Farm folks who had been caravanning together, eating together, smoking together, and therefore knew each other pretty well, were the founding members of the community.

But, things change. People move out to move in with their lover. People have to get out of town for a job or to address health issues of a loved one or simply to move having been disenchanted with shared housing. It's not for everyone. And then, you have to replace those people, particularly if you're not a Trustafarian, living on Daddy & Mommy's money, but are actually on a budget and need a certain amount of rent coming in to pay the bills. So where do you meet these potential new house members?

Some housing co-ops put up notices at health food stores, massage and yoga studios, local organic food outlets or wherever alternative-lifestyle devotees and hippies frequent. Some groups post vacancies on social media. Some simply ask current members to spread the word and trust word of mouth to reach the right people. Hint: Word of mouth works best.

Our experience has shown that always – make that ALWAYS – there are people out there who are looking for safe, affordable housing and community. The trick is connecting with the right ones.

And who are the "right ones?" They are those who seem to already be part of your flock. Seem to be flying in the same direction. The "right ones" simply feel... right. At Hanger Hall, as BD, I interview any potential new housemates; and what I look for is **groundedness** and **flexibility**.

Groundedness:
Do they have some kind of daily direction?
Some kind of clear goal which they are actively pursuing?
...and...
Flexibility:
Do they understand that their way is not the only way?
That there are multitudinous paths, lifestyles, and
orientations, and the gig is to work, play, and
cooperate with each other?

The No-Way-Jose—the one you don't want in your community—is the one who

- gushes negativity
- spouts disparagement at ethnicity, religion, race or any age group
- sniggers with overt sexualization of men or women
- shrugs constantly with a "whatever" attitude

or...

- is unwaveringly OCD and must have all things a certain way
- shares a my-way-or-the-highway attitude about religion, sex, politics
- feels pushy right off the bat
- an overtly sexual prude or player

The Come-On-Inner—the one you want—is the one who

- has a clear sense of humor and an easy smile
- exhibits gentleness and kindness
- is eager to get to know the other residents
- feels like a faucet and not a drain

or...

- shows a clear respect for different religions, styles of living, and sexual orientations
- wants to know what the household needs and how he/she might help
- is not a know-it-all
- is eager to learn how to be an integral part of the community

Some co-ops may choose to have each member meet with the new prospect and decide on membership with a vote. Some may have written agreements that they ask each new resident to sign. The thing to remember is that it's easier to welcome a newbie than to toss them out. Once they're accepted, then getting them to leave can be painful for everyone. It's easier to say, "No" earlier than later. And the damage that a troublesome newbie can do to the community ain't ever pretty. So, choose well.

For a while here at The Hall, we did 30-day trials and if, after that month, it seemed to be working for the community and the newbie, then they were welcomed as solid members. If not, we asked the newbie to move on and we went looking again.

After Hanger Hall had been around for 10-15 years, we started getting so many requests to move in that we made a waiting list. Not wise. We ended up with 30-40 people on the list; and by the time we had an opening, most of the people on the list had already found housing.

These days, we usually get about a call/a week asking if we have space. So, our current method is to interview the potential housemates, invite them to dinner a few times and then ask them to check in every few weeks to see if a room has opened up.

Choosing a new housemate can be tricky. Sometimes, negative behaviors only show up later; and you can never guess when or how. Likewise, some newbies feel "iffy" early on and then blossom later. One thing is very clear, however, once a new person moves in, the entire household changes – sometimes in subtle ways, sometimes dramatically. Every new person adds something new to the entire community. But, if the community is strong and welcoming and clear on boundaries and.... maintains a sense of humor... so friggin' important... chances are that each newbie will feel welcomed, acknowledged, and ready to contribute in making the co-op a joyful place to live.

Chapter 7

In my years here at Hanger Hall,
my biggest take-away is that we are very fortunate
to have someone so well suited
to keeping it running
and also that we have been fortunate
to have some really lovely people living here
who have made the experience
incredibly fun.
It has been a nearly perfect place
to feel the connectedness
of a loose-knit community
of open-minded folks,
without having to give up too much autonomy.

Solon Smith, 2011 –

CHAPTER 8

CLEANLINESS IS NEXT TO... IMPOSSIBLE?

NEATNIKS & SLOBS REVISITED

In Chapter 2, you may have read, *Everyone is responsible for keeping the common areas uncluttered; and the head of household is responsible for maintaining cleanliness.* If you haven't read that or did read it and forgot it, no problem. Here it is again in bold: ***Everyone is responsible for keeping the common areas uncluttered; and the head of household is responsible for maintaining cleanliness.*** Words to live by, Kemosabe. If you ever have anything to do with shared living, these are the words of The Lord.

Our experience at Hanger Hall is that most folks like things fairly tidy and pretty damn clean. Even if you are comfortable waddling around in your own garbage, chances are, you are not willing to do your dance in someone else's pile. So, once again, the holy writ: *Everyone is responsible for keeping the common areas uncluttered; and the head of household is responsible for maintaining cleanliness.*

So, how do you do that? Besides using whips, thumbscrews or threatening to play Justin Bieber every day at breakfast, how do you get everyone on board with keeping the place clean? A few ideas:

1. Leaders – whether you be a BD or not, it is your job to set the example. Without walking the walk, you can talk your ass off and not make a doodle of difference. If your housemates acknowledge you as their leader and see you cleaning on a daily basis, chances are, they will follow your example no matter how many rules and regulations you come up with.
2. Make it clear from the start – before a newbie ever moves in – that cleanliness and tidiness are important. That no matter what the newbie's personal hygiene and home-care habits might be, in the common areas of this house is keeping it happy. Make that abundantly clear!!!
3. Keep humorous reminders here and there in the form of notes of:

- how enticing a clean home smells
- how your chances of getting some action this weekend are a direct corollary of how clean the place is
- how unkempt homes tend to attract flies, rats and exes.

With aides-mémoires, the point is, Keep It Light. Keep It Fun. Keep it Giggly and your chances of keeping a clean house skyrocket.

4. Make a list of daily and/or weekly cleaning gigs, post in a prominent place and leave space under each gig for a resident to initial when they have done their deed. Then, being obvious who's doing what and who's not doing anything, allow social pressure to work its wonders.
5. If the list ain't working and the cleaning ain't happenin', suggest to the group that maybe it might be easier to raise the

rent and hire someone to come in. That job list might just come alive. If not...

6. Hire someone. Could be someone in the house, could be from the outside. Outsiders usually work best. Could work either way; but it is the job of the leader to make sure the job is done. And well.
7. Leaders take a regular (weekly, maybe) tour of the common areas of the house to make sure that things are being kept in good shape; and while on the tour, do a little cleaning yourself. (See Item #1)

That said, even acknowledging the magnitude of importance with the cleaning department, when it comes to shared duties, there are still much bigger fish to fry. Paraphrasing my favorite author, Tom Robbins, "If godliness isn't next to something more interesting than cleanliness, it might be time to reevaluate our notions of godliness."

WHO DOES WHAT? – DOIN' WHAT COMES NATURALLY

When a newbie moves in, a good question to ask is, "Is there a particular element of house-cleaning or maintenance that you enjoy doing more than others?" Then ask if they would be willing to help with that. Chances are... especially if they want to move in... they will answer in the affirmative.

Ideally, each person in a shared housing situation wants each other person to be happy. Ideally. And, of course, things are not always ideal. But everyone - except for the masochistic meathead - wants to be happy themselves. So, if you are doing a chore in which you take pleasure... or like...or at least put up with while maintaining a positive attitude, then your happiness is not jeopardized; while at the same time, in doing that chore, you are bumping up the happiness quotient of everyone in the house.

For example:

- At Hanger Hall, there are people who enjoy emptying the dishwasher. OK, maybe "enjoy" is a bit over the top; but some people would rather put away clean dishes than wash dirty ones.
- At Hanger Hall, there are people who really like a well-scrubbed bathtub or shower. Others could care less.
- Some folks actually don't mind taking out the garbage, recycling or compost. Or, if they do mind, they are so gagged by the rancid smell of the long-forgotten mold-covered meatloaf, they readily volunteer.
- Some folks like to vacuum their room every few days. Others don't even know what a vacuum cleaner looks like. If they love vacuuming, they'll probably do the common areas.
- Basically no one likes to clean the toilets. No one. But a majority of people would rather poop in a clean porcelain pot rather than a porta potty look-alike. God knows what might be living and waiting down there to jump up and bite your whoopee-cakes. Not to mention the aroma-therapy that comes with a filthy pot. And in a shared housing situation, it doesn't take long -- not long at all -- for a good clean toilet to start looking and smelling like its Job-Johnny cousin. So, cleaning the toilet needs to be a shared task and a sign above the pot with room for initials and a date can encourage that volunteerism.
- Some people are fix-it meisters. Handymen or women. People who love tools and usually come with a neat little satchel of pliers, screwdrivers, box-cutters, hammers, saws, scrapers,

sandpaper, chisels, staple guns, tape measures, and often, a neat little plastic box filled with all sizes of screws, nuts, bolts and picture hangers. If they love doing it, chances are they'll be glad to do it throughout the house.

- Some people can't stand cobwebs. Show them the broom.
- Some people love clean windows. Let them know where the Windex and paper towels live.
- Some people love working outside. Point them towards the rake, the shovel, the leaf blower, the lawn mower.

The idea here is clear. You get it. People would rather do what they like to do; and if what they like to do benefits the entire community, it's a win, win, win, win, win.... situation.

PICKING YOUR BATTLES & PICKING YOUR NOSE

Why do gorillas have big nostrils?
Because they have big fingers.

Most folks pick their noses. Deny it, though they may, I have seen nose-pickers from all walks of life. Some do it delicately with a hanky or tissue; but they're still picking. Some less tactfully with a quick insertion and swipe of the pinky finger. Some dig in and go for it like an archaeologist in a manner that would make any 5-year old proud.

Likewise, some folks pick their noses only on rare occasions like upon returning from an all-day camel ride in the Sahara. Some pick it more regularly, just before going into a meeting or prior to a first date or when you're driving alone and stuck in traffic. I have witnessed more rush-hour nose pickers than in any section of humanity. Other than a kindergarten class. Some, I am pretty certain, pick their noses out of habit: a kind of addiction like smoking or movie popcorn or beef jerky and corn nuts on road trips. For these folks, a finger in the nostril is not just about boogers, but about comfort. Frisky Finger snuggling with Nanny Nostril.

Despite varieties of style and frequency and depth of plunder, however, most folks in Western Civilization tend to pick their noses in private. They get the job done; but are not big on sharing the event with the world. Except for the rush-hour bunch who could care less.

"So what has this to do," you might ask, "with shared housing?" I haven't a clue. Just thought we needed a little diversion. Heh-heh.

Actually, there is an analogy. Sort of.

In any community of people, be it a nuclear family, a couple, a classroom, an office or a living co-op, there are boogers (aka nasty issues) which need to be addressed. Problems which need to be tackled, troubles which need to be dealt with. And there are different ways of dealing with them.

- Some prefer to leave most problems (aka boogers) alone hoping they'll take care of themselves. And sometimes, that works.
- Some choose to deal with them on a fairly regular basis with the thought that nipping a booger (aka problem) in the bud will keep it from growing and becoming a bigger challenge. And sometimes, that is effective.
- And then, there are some who are always digging around for some boogery issue or challenge with which to deal. And that is almost always a big mistake.

Is the booger analogy working?

In any event, most folks choose not to deal with problems out in the open for all to see. Which is right up there with Confucius-level wisdom. Dragging your community's problems (boogers) out for all to see is tantamount to mounting an arms race to create peace. Or having sex to promote virginity.

Most problems in a community involve only one or two persons. Intrapersonal squabbles come with the territory. They are as inevitable as boogers. Sometimes there are issues which involve the whole community:

- the hot water heater goes on the fritz,
- the roof leak has gotten worse,
- someone keeps leaving the tea kettle on till it's boiled dry,
- out of toilet paper or someone used half-a-roll with one flush and the plunger has gone missing, etc.

By and large, most problems I have encountered in 4+ decades of shared housing involve only 1-3 persons. And, like picking your nose, these situations are always best handled (so to speak) privately.

Everyone in Hanger Hall Co-op is 18 or older. So, since everyone is an adult, I choose to treat each one as an adult. If there are personality struggles, I remind the contenders of their adultness and encourage each of them to deal with it. As an adult. I am not – nor will I ever choose to be, *in loco parentis*. The name "loco" says it all. In our housing co-op, I am not anyone's daddy or mommy. I am the BD of the household and an encouraging friend to each member. Leaders of any shared housing community can burn out faster than a shooting star if he or she tries to solve everyone's problems. Or pick everyone's noses...just to keep the analogy going.

If you are a leader – or potential leader – of a living co-op, my best advice is to trust people to pick their own noses. In private. Do not...do not...for Goddess' sake...do not always go looking for problems – for boogers to pick. When noses are picked too much, they bleed. Same for the community.

Every now and then, however, one or two or three people can, by their own struggles and frustrations, affect the whole community. When you live closely with one another and the water is stirred, the ripples affect everyone. Whether it's joyful or sorrowful ripples, giddy or anguished ripples, everyone gets touched and it finally affects the life of the community. Hence, choose carefully which boogers you want to deal with and which you trust will take care of themselves. My choice has always been to deal only with issues that have spilled over and have started to affect the entire community. Other than that, I trust each person to...pick their own noses. Just go get a tissue and shut up about it.

PETS

A couple who lived with us for many years had a cat. They loved their kitty. They treated it as their child and would even talk to the cat as if they were the parent. "Do you want mommy to fix you something good for dinner?" etc. Not my style; but some people do adore their pets immensely.

This cat, however, found its way into the room of one of our members - a member who happened to be a musician and made his living - and a pretty decent living it was - playing guitar and singing. This musician was not necessarily fond of cats or dogs; but he was OK with his housemates venerating their cat. The cat, however, while he was in the musician's room, peed in the musician's open guitar case. That, let's just say, didn't go over well. The couple who owned the cat apologized profusely and tried ever so unsuccessfully to remove the smell from the guitar case.

At another time, it happened that three of our residents had big dogs, as in big, Labrador/Golden Retriever/German Shepherd type dogs.

(A minister friend of mine has a German Shepherd which she named "Lord." And now she can honestly say, "The Lord is my shepherd.")

And these three dogs, of course, loved to follow their owners around. Which was fine. Except when all three residents and their dogs came into the kitchen. Anyone else who came into the kitchen to cook during that time, whether he or she loved dogs or not, had to deal with flying fur, slippery slobber, unabashed begging and wanton woofs while scrambling their eggs. We learned a lesson: kitchens are kitchens and kennels are kennels. Period.

These days, individual pet owners keep their pets in their rooms or on a leash. No free-roaming-guitar-case-pissing-kitchen-crowding animals in the house allowed. And everyone's cool with that.

The goal of living in a cooperative is to cooperate. It's simple. It's challenging. But it can be done. And, perhaps, someday, we will learn to do that on a global scale.

CHILDREN

You're only young once, but you can be immature forever.

There are many, many single moms and dads in the world and, though I've seen no research on this, my impression is that the vast majority of single parents have very little money. Or time. So, inexpensive housing and child care are two of their top priorities. Enter Cooperative Housing. It's usually inexpensive, or at least far less than standard single-family housing. That's the good news. The bad news is: everyone loves kids. Except the ones who don't. And there are those.

For many folks, it's not so much a dislike for children as it is a preference for adult company. When children are around, dynamics change. Adult conversation is redirected or curtailed. Nor are we just talking sex here. OK, sex talk is part of what gets redirected. But simple conversation on what happened at the job today or what's on the news or trying to find a new focus for living can get awkward in the presence of kids. Particularly if they're not your kids.

Likewise, kids generally have a lot of energy. Eveready Bunny, eat your heart out. So you get home from a long day, pull out a cold one, plop your weary self onto the couch and in come a couple of 8 year-olds screaming through the front door and doing an Indianapolis 500 around the living room. In such a situation, Gandhi might say, "Kids will be kids." But you're not Gandhi. So what comes out is, "Shut the F*** up!" Which you're immediately sorry for. Sort of.

It might well take a village to raise a child; but preferably one with a well-stocked wine cellar. Barring that, unless the members of the household have understood from the start that children might be part of the picture, you can't expect your village to do the raising. It is very true that, in any community, living with elders and children help humanize the whole scene. But when the elders and children are not your own, it's a different story.

Our experience over the decades has shown that children are not an overall plus in shared housing. We have accommodated children in our home from time to time, but over the long haul, there are more problems than blessings.

If, however you decide to include children in your co-op, I would suggest a few guidelines:

- The children should never be given free, unsupervised reign of the house.
- The children should be taught clearly the same boundaries and restrictions which everyone follows.
- No parent should ever expect his/her housemates to automatically watch over or discipline a child simply because they live in the same house.

Living at Hanger Hall was an amazing time for me,
like a second college dorm experience,
but with finer furnishings
and less rules.
I moved in when I was 24, and stayed until age 31.
The community of people evolved as I lived there,
and each iteration was unique unto itself.

The best part was the traditions
we created together-
the fireside and poolside dinners,
hanging stockings
and dying Easter eggs.
There was always a kind ear and a hot meal,
a New York times Crossword in the kitchen
and comforting constant energy.
When I lived at Hanger Hall,
I didn't go out as much.
Most of my social needs were met at home.

I found my place in that big house.
And to this day it still feels like home.

Cara Steinbuchel 2005 – 2012

CHAPTER 9

OWNERSHIP

RESIDENTIAL vs ABSENTEE OWNERSHIP

Never having operated a Living Co-op with a lease arrangement, my observations are limited. I have always owned Hanger Hall and always lived here. When I traveled with my band, I might be gone for a couple of months; but, by far and away, I have lived most of my days in the home.

I have, however, owned additional rental property outside of Hanger Hall; and can clearly come down on the positive side of residential ownership. Rental properties – whether a car, boat, house, B&B, whatever -- are never, ever given high quality care if the owner is not directly involved. When you don't own something and are simply using it temporarily, you have no personal connection to it. No sense of ownership. It's simply a "thing." An "it." But, when the owner is an active part of the home, members feel more connected. Even though everyone knows that legally the house is owned by someone else, the fact that that particular someone else is living there with you offers an emotional connection to the property that you don't have otherwise.

When something goes wrong with our building, residents will help out to make it right. With repairs, I always foot the bill, of course; but it is obvious that each resident has an individual stake in maintaining the structure. It's home for us all.

Years back, a freak tornado (tornados tend to be more fond of wide open spaces and mobile homes than mountains and mansions) ripped off the roof of our kitchen. It also happened to be pouring rain. Immediately after the tornado had passed, everyone - literally, everyone - jumped in to help with moving refrigerators, clearing out cabinets, mopping floors, moving buckets, emptying pails, crawling up on the roof with tarps and on and on and on into the night. And with everyone's help, we were even able to fix and enjoy breakfast in a semi-dry kitchen the very next morning. The replacement roof, of course, took a bit longer. But thebreakfast was good.

Don't know if that would have happened had we all been renting and the owner didn't live there. Maybe it would have. But my guess is that, after we freaked out and called the owner, many of us would have gathered our personal kitchen stuff and run up to our rooms or a nearby hotel.

If residential ownership is not possible, my suggestion would be to make good friends with the owner. Invite the owner over for dinner or drinks on a regular basis as a way of personalizing the home and allowing it to become a place not just for the body, but for the heart - a place where each member of household feels a sense of ownership. There's something about being connected with the owner that connects you with what is owned.

RIGHTS & PRIVILEGES

I raised two daughters in our Hanger Hall Cooperative. For 20 years. From birth to college. And they made it through mostly unscathed. Nothing that a few years of therapy can't handle. Actually, they are both astounding young women. I know, it sounds like Daddy-brag and it is. Suck it up! But each of these amazing young women have said over and over that growing up in shared housing actually taught them how to relate to non-familial adults far better than had they grown up with just Mom or Dad.

Their mother, my former wife, was part of the household until she and I divorced when the kids were ages seven and nine. She was an active member of our tribe and contributed wonderfully to its success.

Everyone in the house, of course, was aware that my kids and wife were family, and as such might expect special treatment. And, on the one hand, that was so. Neither my children nor my wife ever paid rent and each had her room. On the other hand, each of us was expected to follow the flow and guidelines of the house. We

- honored 10 p.m. -7 a.m. quiet times
- folded any laundry we took from the dryer
- helped load and unload the dishwasher
- cleaned and tidied any common space we had used
- swept or vacuumed as needed
- greeted each person we met
- joined in on our house dinners along with cooking and cleaning
- and yada yada yada....

In other words, my family was acknowledged as being "special," but was also an active and integral part of the Co-op.

But wait a minute! What about the whole No-Kids thing?

As George Orwell pegged it, "All animals are equal, but some are more equal than others." In any social situation, there is a pecking order. In a work environment, it could be based on job ranking. In a family environment, it's usually based on age and parental authority. At school, it's the teachers and administrators who are top dogs. At a party, looks, clothes, wealth and personality often take upper drawer. In shared housing, it's usually seniority. Those who have lived there the longest automatically assume top dog status. They know the protocol, they know the history, they know what is expected, they know what's what. And what isn't what. And as existential-sounding as that may be, the senior members of a shared housing household are usually the wisdom keepers. They become the go-tos for the newbies. And they are either tacitly or blatantly acknowledged as the guides and sages. And the truth of the matter is that they do serve that function.

At Hanger Hall, we have had a man living with us for 3 decades. He is our oldest resident. Early on, he occupied several different rooms, but over half of his life in The Hall has been in The Tower – the tippy-top of the mansion. Primo rooms. It's like living in a tree house. He is an extremely active part of the household community. He loves to fix things and is good at it. Plumbing, electrical, furniture. He is affable, easy to laugh with and highly respected in the house as the eldest of our elders. His seniority and consistently helpful involvement with the entire household have perched him way up high in the pecking order in our home.

Every society demands structure; and the two essential structures for every culture are organization and community. Both are necessary. But one is a necessary evil. As David Stindl-Rast suggested in one of his books, organization must exist for any group of people to operate together. But, organization has no heart, and as such, can trample on community. And even destroy it. It is the job of any community to develop healthy organization and then, be its watchdog - never allowing it to get so big and powerful that it destroys the very community it was engaged to enhance.

Seniority is part of the structure not only in shared housing, but in business, military and academics. It's why teachers and professors bust ass to achieve tenure. It's why middle management employees work and schmooze their butts off to rise in the office hierarchy. It's why young army officers put in ridiculously long hours, while bowing and scraping to their superiors, hoping to get a shot at moving up the ranks.

You, O Noble Reader, can probably remember either in high school or college when you were a freshman. An **UNDER** classman. You knew that's what you were and if you forgot, you were quickly reminded by the **UPPER** classmen to keep your place. They got in your face so you'd keep your place. It may have seemed unfair from time to time, but chances are, you found a bit of comfort in knowing your place and knowing others that were also in your place and knowing that each of the **UPPER** classmen were once in your place and that someday, you would be an **UPPER** and not an **UNDER.** Just that little bit of upper/under goofiness gives structure to the social life of a school experience, offers organization to what probably felt foreign and confusing, and usually enriches school life by offering a sense of comfort and belonging.

Rights and privileges in shared housing - whether by seniority, leadership or ownership - can enhance the sense of security for all, provided that it does not undermine community and the sense of connection with each and every individual. Senior members and leaders of a shared housing community deserve recognition and privileges and at the same time should be expected to share their knowledge, experience and lead the way in making that community the most functional, happy and dynamic collective possible. Hence, my children were fully accepted in the house.

OVERSTEPPING THE BOUNDS

Newbies and veterans each have a role to play in any shared housing experience. Newbies have a learning curve to navigate and veterans have a responsibility to lead by example. But, since people are people and human nature is human nature and laziness is laziness and pride is pride and...well, you get the picture...it doesn't always work that way.

We had a senior member awhile back who was constantly criticizing the newbies. He wouldn't slam them with a straight-up verbal slap; but rather play the passive/aggressive game. "I remember when our toilets used to be kept sparkling clean," he would say when a couple of newbies were around. "I don't know what has happened." Or, "Damn! I can't find anything in the kitchen anymore. Doesn't anyone know where things belong?" Or, "Wish some folks would learn that if you leave your clothes in the washer overnight, they could mildew?" And so on. And sometimes, he would blow off at a newbie with a, "Look, I've been here for five years. Have seen a lot of people come and go. Can't you get you act together?"

The boy was no fun to live with; and it wasn't long before he and we all realized that he simply was not a happy man and was taking it out on his housemates. He moved on of his own accord.

Then, at another time, we had a newbie who assumed that the veterans were gurus. All kinds of gurus. Especially relationship gurus. "I know you've lived in this community for a long time," she would begin. "It's my first time and it brings up all these traumatic memories of past boyfriends. Could we just talk?" Which was fine. For a bit. That's what happens when you live together. You talk about stuff. But this young woman appeared to assume that our home was some kind of relationship rehab unit and she would "talk" with each one as if we were her therapists.

She would sometimes sit and drink coffee at the kitchen table when she wasn't at work or in school, and whenever anyone came in to grab a quick bite, she would launch into her current repertoire of life's troubles. "See, I've been hanging out with this guy lately and he's really cute and all; but then yesterday, my old boyfriend who I really loved but who dumped me...anyway, so he calls and says...." And on and on. The person who just came in the kitchen may have just wanted a PBJ. Instead, he or she was treated to an elaborate stir-fry of hormonal misery. Not a healthy M.O. And finally, someone in the house had a "talk" with her and told her that, as none of us were counselors and were not getting paid for listening, we were getting tired of constantly hearing about her problems. She actually paid attention and decided to get a real therapist.

Suffice it to say that a Living Cooperative is just that – a group of people striving to live together cooperatively. That's it. No one is there to fix anyone else or to convince anyone else that they need fixing. No one is there to convert, cajole, sweet-talk or inveigle anyone to be anyone other than who they are. Unless, of course, they are not living cooperatively. If someone is being a jerk, they need to be reminded that respect is the bottom line; though everyone is entitled to be a jerk every now and then. If someone is feeling needy, what they truly need is a reminder that the house is not an assisted living facility. Not a therapeutic asylum. But everyone feels needy every now and then. Everyone needs a hug or a listening ear here and there. It's a balance. Always a balance. Living together requires a patient and kind effort on everyone's part to be part of the balancing act.

Truly the house is a gem,
a marvel
and full of magic.
The part that most amazed me was the kitchen.
Howard has unlocked the secret to communal living,
by insisting all dishes
get washed immediately after cooking
and when they don't,
he pulls up the slack and sweeps the kitchen Zen-like
every AM at 6.

Hanger Hall is a true joy and wonder and mystery.
It's magic goes beyond
and through
the present generation
to the founders and into the future.

It's a joy and privilege to live there...
until my share of the winter heat bill comes due.

Laeo McDermott, 2015

CHAPTER 10

PRIVACY

A close musician friend of mine who lives half-way across the country, has come to visit me many times over the years. We always have a good time when he's here; but at some time during almost every visit, he says, "I could never live with a bunch of people like you do. I need a lot more privacy."

It's true: Cooperative living is less private than when you have your own home. In co-op housing, even though you have your own room where no one enters unless invited, once you leave that room, you enter common spaces where any and everyone in the house are always welcome.

In your own private non-co-op home, you might wake up at night and stroll butt-naked to the kitchen to get some left-over pizza and a slurp of wine. No problem. But in a co-op, if you do that, you might be welcomed in your butt-nakedness by another couple of residents and maybe two of their guests having a midnight snack themselves. Not a necessarily positive experience for anyone.

In your own home, if you feel like dancing at 2:00 in the morning, you could cue up your iPod, Bluetooth some speakers, ramp up the volume and dance the night away. In a co-op, you will likely have no dance partners, but may well have several vocal nay-sayers. Very vocal nay-sayers.

In your own home, if you're having a romantic evening and things get hot and hoppin', you can have some fun on the dining table or the living room couch or the chandelier (has anyone really swung naked on a chandelier?); but in a co-op, chances are you'll not only be coitally interrupted but might even see some compromising pix of yourself and your beloved on FaceBook the next day.

Co-op living lacks total privacy, indeed. And therefore, it is vital that whatever privacy exists in your shared home is honored and respected diligently. When you only got a little, you make the best of that little. It's true in multiple situations.

At Hanger Hall, barring an emergency, we do not ever go into another person's room without their express permission. If the resident of a particular room is not at home, that room is just as private as if he or she were present. There are exceptions, of course. One night, we smelled smoke and went quickly from room to room tracking it down. But even at that, we always knocked and called, just in case the resident was sleeping. Turned out, it was coming from a bonfire in the neighborhood. Another time, one of our residents was out for the evening and had inadvertently set his uber-loud boom box to turn on at 11:00 p.m. to keep his dog amused. After knocking like a jack hammer on his door and trying to text him for permission, I went in and turned down the sleep-snatcher.

At The Hall, we have several conversation areas where people can gather and chatter and drink. Or just chatter. Or just drink. However, even though these are common spaces, sometimes the conversation gets intimate; and it doesn't take a Carl Jung to figure that out. People in our house are very aware that if the conversation going on in these areas feels private, you give some space. Our front porch has 6 nice rocking chairs; but if an intense conversation or make-out session is going on in any of those chairs, others in the house know to wait and rock later.

Personal space must be absolutely honored in a shared housing situation. It should be honored anywhere, of course; but in shared housing, where the space is already limited, it behooves each resident to honor every other resident with as much privacy as possible.

PERSONAL PROPERTY

We had a visitor once at Hanger Hall who assumed that we were a commune - a classic-share-everything-you-got commune. So we caught him again and again going through residents' cabinets and refrigerator space, eating their food and even stuffing munchies in his backpack for a hike. We asked him to cease and desist. He told us we were being selfish and should share. We told him he was fast becoming persona non-grata. Just as we never go into another's room without permission, nor do we eat -- or even borrow -- someone else's food without their consent.

Everyone who lives in our house would get a "shares well with other children" comment on their report card; but we are still, each and all, products of Western Civilization's dictum that possession is 9/10 of the law and perhaps 10/10 of human relationships. We are, for good or ill, part and parcel of a consumer culture; and we likes what we owns, so a pure Oneida communalism (Chapter1) just don't work for us. We highly respect personal property from Beanie-Weenies to Bob Marley albums to Bose headphones to bloomers. Especially bloomers.

We do have a place in our kitchen called, "The Zone." Anything that appears in The Zone (it's almost always food) is up for grabs. If you come home with more pizza than you can handle, you can leave it in The Zone. If you're cleaning out your cabinet and find four cans of pickled pig's feet which you bought for some ganja-inspired and ganja-forgotten casserole...you can take 'em to The Zone.

Over the years, many later night revelers have come in from party or movie, and, to their delight, found a midnight snack in The Zone far better than anything on the Denny's menu. Once, a resident attended a relative's wedding and came back at 2:00 in the morning with kitchen leftovers from an apparently Bacchanalian wedding feast: prime rib, roasted veggies, mac-n-cheese, potatoes au gratin and enough fresh baked rolls and croissants to keep China's triathlon team in carbs till the 2nd Coming of Confucius. Needless to say, the next morning breakfast was a whole new experience.

In the end, privacy and respect for personal property is pivotal in any shared community. People who have been robbed -- either through mugging, burglary or whatever -- often refer to the experience as "having been violated." It's a frightening and debasing thing to happen to anyone. And though having a housemate come in your room to borrow a shirt or get into your food cabinet and make a PBJ or open the fridge and eat your ice cream is not the same as a personal assault, you can, nonetheless, feel violated and, at the very least, disrespected. Actually, in my way of thinking, someone eating your ice cream is definitely a personal assault. And if they eat it all, it's a bona fide crime.

Chapter 10

RELATIONSHIPS, SEX & EMOTIONAL SPACE

There is only one thing worse than being talked about and that is not being talked about.
- Oscar Wilde

When you eat breakfast together with several people or brush your teeth in the same sink with them or poo in the same pot or play games or go out drinking together...when you live with the same people day after day, conversations happen. All kinds of conversations. And often -- very often – that chatter is about relationships. Personal relationships. Who's involved with whom? How deeply? What happened to that last partner? Where are they now? Who's the new hottie? Are they sleeping together? And so on and on and on.

Relationship talk comes naturally and can offer some spicy fun. Checking out who's currently with whom and who is history and who you heard at 3:00 this a.m. either throwing punches or thumpin' thighs, can be at least as entertaining as FaceBook. But the problem with relationship tête-à-tête often teeters on the brink of gossipy-goop. Gossip can be destructive, especially when you live with the gossiper and gossipee. No one likes to be talked about in derogatory or disparaging ways. No one likes his or her sex life laid on the examination table for all to see. And, though it might seem like giddy, innocent chatter, hurt feelings are often the result.

Every now and then, there will be a couple in the house who are particularly boisterous and vocal when it comes to the horizontal hula. It doesn't take long living together to be aware of what sounds travel how far in the house. So, in almost every case of a jammin' mattress dance in our house, the dancers emerge the next morning with a knowing grin that they had provided some entertainment the previous night. No behind-the-back prattle; just straight-up smirking acknowledgement by all of the happy erotic boom-booms from the prior night.

One woman in our house had, over the years, achieved such a reputation for her "orgasmic arias," as she called them, that she would even give us fair warning that another opera might soon be in the works. One evening, about eight of us were together at dinner; and it happened that her room was directly above the dining room. At mid-dinner, the curtain evidently went up in the room above us, the lust and thrust was in full swing and the lovely diva erupted in song. Each of us with a huge grin, looked around the table and with nary an encouraging word all went up the stairs, gathered outside her door and when the aria came to an ever-so-apparent climax, applauded exultantly. She and her man friend came to the door, opened it and with a single sheet – or was it a window curtain – wrapped around them both, they bowed deeply as we continued to cheer. Living together can foster that kind of delicious frivolity.

At Hanger Hall, we have come to realize the value of honoring each other's personal space, personal food and personal lives. Likewise, we celebrate our resident's positive relationships and are willing to listen or perhaps simply empathize when relationships take a tumble. For the most part, we are pretty open about discussing our love and family lives with each other; but when someone needs a bit of distance or wishes not to talk, we have learned to back off.

Every now and then at The Hall, you come into the kitchen and find a person crying or clearly upset. "Do you need a hug?" is often a good entrée for such a situation. And sometimes, the answer is "yes" and sometimes, "no." But when any expression of care and concern is offered by another house-mate, it reaffirms community. Reasserts the importance of compassion. Reiterates the sense of closeness, safety and respect which undergirds any successful shared housing. Kindness and compassion are never out of place.

VISITORS

After three days, both fish and visitors smell.
Mark Twain, Ben Franklin, Confucius, Jesus... who knows?

It's important to remember that each of your housemates is connected to a galaxy of other people: friends, ex-friends, lovers, ex-lovers, family, family they wish weren't, former hook-ups, potential hook-ups, unfortunate hook-ups, golf partners, running cohorts, marathon meet-uppers, business buddies, employers, employees... I read somewhere that the average US citizen can name 67 people with whom he or she would consider to be closely connected. So, unless your housemates are all introverted hermit-wanna-bes, chances are, each of them will entertain some members of their galaxies at some point – or at several points – while they are living with you.

Visitors can be delightful in a living co-op. Visitors provide variety: new topics of conversation, new ways of thinking, new philosophies and of course, new faces. Visitors can offer insight into the housemate they are visiting. After a visitor leaves, if you paid attention, you will be aware of new ways of seeing and knowing your housemate who entertained the visitor.

Visitors can also be challenging: Where do they sleep? Where do they hang out when their visitee is at work or school? Do they understand the house rules about smoking, pets, sharing food, time spent in the bathroom, etc?

At Hanger Hall, if it's not OK – for whatever reason – for a visitor to stay in the housemate's room, we have an office space with a fold-out (and dreadfully uncomfortable) couch. 'Tis the nature of fold-out couches. My theory is that people buy fold-out couches for their guests as a way of insuring that the guests will not stay for more than a night or two. My other theory is that fold-out couches were designed by chiropractors as job security. I highly recommend fold-out couches for guests in Co-op Living.

With visitors, we ask for these agreements from the visitee:

- Put up a note or spread the word that a visitor is expected on what date and for how long
- Be sure everyone in the house knows the name of coming visitor
- Make sure the visitor is aware of house rules and the way the house works
- Invite no more than 1-2 visitors at a time without express consent from the other house members
- If the visitor should end up having an extended stay (10 days or more), be sure that they are invited to chip in on utilities, clean-up and maintenance.

Since I grew up at Hanger Hall,
the idea of being raised in a co-living situation
never struck me as out of the ordinary.
Reflecting on my childhood,
I loved being raised by my parents
surrounded by a fun, diverse group
of housemates.
It's hard not to hone your communication skills early on
when your kitchen is a bustling hive
of 5-10 people every morning!
To this day I credit my
extroversion and comfort
in a myriad of social situations
to my "unique" childhood home experience.

Windsor Hanger, 1988 – 2006
Howard's daughter

Chapter 10

CHAPTER 11

THE FUN FACTOR

My faith is whatever makes me feel good about being alive.
If your religion doesn't make you feel good to be alive,
what the hell is the point of it?
Tom Robbins, "Fierce Invalids Home From Hot Climates"

In Day of the Dead (Dia de los Muertos) celebrations throughout Mexico in the first few days of November, one of the traditions is to paint half of a celebrant's face as a skull while leaving the other half untouched. Half-living, Half-dead. The point is to remind one and all that it's but a fine line between life and death - that the skull of death is just behind skin and eyes. And so it is vital to live as fully as possible in every moment. As poet Mary Oliver puts it:

Doesn't everything die at last, and too soon?
Tell me, what is it you plan to do
with your one wild and precious life?

- "The Summer Day" from "New and Selected Poems, Volume 1"

And, since we spend a whoppin' big chunk of our time on this planet in the place where we live, if we are wise, we would make that place and experience as full of life as possible. When the place you live becomes no more than a sleep-and-eat station or a place to wash your butt and your underwear—however important that may be—then we're missing a grand and glorious opportunity to own and relish a huge segment of our lives. Where we live...where we make and call our home...where we come to refresh, rejuvenate and recharge...where we know we are accepted and appreciated...this place—wherever it may be for you—is absolutely crucial for a full and joyful, wild and precious life.

Whether you live alone or with 15 others doesn't really matter. What does matter is your quality of life. If death is indeed just round the corner for each of us, doesn't it make sense to keep this side of the corner as filled with pleasure, satisfaction and kindness as possible? Chances are you spend more of your waking and sleeping hours in your home than anywhere else. No matter how joyless your job might be, no matter how you may struggle with finances, family, or relationships, having a home that nurtures and feeds your soul can bump up your quality of life in ways nothing else can.

Shared housing offers some particularly unique attributes for improving any life. Living with diverse personalities and philosophies, assorted tastes in food and humor...living with people who read different books than you, watch different movies than you, listen to different music, have different sexual orientations, different ways of relating or not relating to The Divine...and knowing that each and every one has essentially the same human desires as you, including: love, acceptance, forgiveness, purpose, peace and joy. This healthy mix can enhance a life like nothing else.

So, if you decide to move in together with one or two or more, never forget that one of the most fundamental foundations of a healthy household is fun. Gladness. Delight. Pleasure. Transcending and understanding differences comes easily with laughter. With laughter, dissimilarities become blessings. With laughter, chores lighten up. Laughter is said to help digest your food. But, in truth, that's only the beginning. Deep belly laughs can help you digest the problems of the day, the worries of the week, the anxiety and fretfulness that we each generate on any average day. Laughter helps it all go down and out much easier, allowing the body, heart and soul to digest – to take from life what will feed you and to dump and flush the rest.

I cannot overestimate the value laughter has played over the decades in this Living Cooperative we call Hanger Hall. Laughter has helped heal wounds of heart and mind. Of broken promises and relationships. And, I'm pretty sure it has even contributed to the healing of bodies as well. Whoever said, "Laughter is the best medicine," and "She who laughs lasts" and "A laugh a day keeps the doctor away," had something going on.

If I had any one thing to suggest for people living together, 'twould be laughter. OK, along with stability, kindness, flexibility and, of course, cleanliness.

Let's move in together.

Growing up at Hanger Hall has helped me learn
not just how to get along with others,
but how to connect with others.
The constant flow of people in and out
and ever changing dynamic nature of the house
has somehow never changed the basis
of what Hanger Hall is all about.
At the weekly "house dinner",
it really feels like you are eating with family,
a weird and eclectic family,
but family.

Chapter 11

I am grateful to have grown up
in such a unique home;
for without a doubt,
it has helped shaped who I am today.

Kelsey Hanger, 1990 - 2008, 2015
(Howard's daughter)

POST SCRIPT

(AKA AFTERTHOUGHTS)

When I was 21 years old, my dad died. When I was 25, I lost my mom. At age 29, I got divorced and moved in to this big house with my band. Had you told me at age 12, 16 or 20 that I would end up living almost my entire adult life with a group of unrelated people, I would have laughed and said something like, "Great imagination! Ever thought about working for Disney?"

But that is precisely what happened. I did move in with my band and have spent every day of my life from then on living with unrelated people. Maybe it was the deaths and divorce that turned the tide; but up until age 29, I was pretty confident that I was on the path to get married, have kids, settle down, be a Methodist minister, pay my taxes, have a mortgage, own a dependable car and live a proper life.

And that "proper life" prospect did not include living with a bunch of unrelated people. Or operating on a shoestring budget. Or smoking dope. Or having multiple girlfriends. Or parties in the hot tub. Or traveling several times around the world playing music for many, many people who could speak ne'r a word of English. That "proper life" prospect did not include sharing a kitchen, bathroom, living room, front porch, back deck, laundry and hot tub rooms with people I had only known for a few years or even a few days. That "proper life" prospect did not match up with almost any aspect of my life from age 29 till today; and yet, I have come to realize that my imagined "proper life" would never have been proper for me.

My housemates have become family for me. Certainly not my only family. I still have sisters and cousins, daughters, son-in-law and grandchildren. I dearly love them all. But my housemates are my live-in family. My day-to-day connection. My consistent link. My reliable community. Do I love my housemates like I love my family? No. There is not - nor will there ever be the blood-marriage-and-time-related depth found in family. But I do love these housemates. They are family. And I value their presence in my life.

Folks move in together for a variety of motives, of course. Some are prompted by romance, some by loneliness, some for financial reasons, some for sharing mutual interests, some because they simply want to live with good friends. Over the 40+ years of living in community, I have discovered that motives don't matter as much as intentions. People come to all kinds of different and sometimes difficult circumstances, but if their intent is to live cooperatively and with integrity, things tend to always work out.

We've had more than few move is with us after a divorce or break-up. They come in unsettled with shattered dreams, sadness and often anger. But, again and again, I have seen that if they live with a sense of teamwork and kindness, they soon find hugs and healing are readily available because we've all been through it, one way or another.

Community is good for that. Anne Lamott, one of my favorite authors, writes, "I do not understand the mystery of grace, only that is meets us where we are but never leaves us where it found us."* Community can do that. Healthy, kind and cooperating community does that. Over and over I have seen people come in to our household feeling broke and broken; and by and by, the smiles return and more and more laughter is heard.

My sense is that our culture and society are hungry for community. We tend to live desperately disparate lives, focused more on all kinds of screens than on others of our kind. The tears, laughter, discussions, perspectives, music and stories with which we connect are almost always digital. Nor am I one of those old fart grumblers who wishes for the "good old days" when kids played baseball instead of video and when teenagers talked rather than texted. I, personally am a fan of Google, Siri and Alexa. But along with all the screens, we need connection: eating together, holding hands, shared tears, mutual belly laughs, hikes in the woods, skinny-dipping in the streams, love-making wherever. Living together provides much-needed connection.

This morning I was in the kitchen with a couple of other residents (aka Hallians) and one of our female Hallians walked in and began wandering around looking in the dishwasher and the cabinets and the refrigerator for whatever. Back and forth. Back and forth. We watched quietly. After a few minutes of this fruitless kitchen circuit, she stopped, looked at us, laughed and said, "I'm glad I live with you guys who don't mind me bumbling around with my pre caffeinated brain. It's nice to be accepted even when you don't know what you're doing."

If this book is about anything, it's about living fully and loving abundantly. So, whether you find yourself in shared housing with 15 sharply-dressed, buttoned-down, shiny-shoes business people in a big old home in New York or living with 12 massage-therapists, acupuncturists, psychics, musicians and aura-readers in Sedona or living with 3 organic kale farmers in a yurt in Montana, or even if you have made a ganja-induced vow to live as a hermit in an abandoned Sears store in Topeka, my wish for you is the same: May you live with kindness, with forgiveness, with joy, with compassion and may you always and forever be open to infinite possibilities.

*Anne LaMott, "Traveling Mercies" Knopf Doubleday